D1459589

SWANSEA LIBRARIES
WITHDRAWN
6000330181

30-SECOND
ROCK MUSIC

30-SECOND
ROCK MUSIC

The 50 key styles, artists and happenings, each explained in half a minute

Editor
Mike Evans

Contributors
Mike Evans
Gillian G. Gaar
Patrick Humphries
Paul Kingsbury
Spencer Leigh
Hugh Weldon

Illustrator
Steve Rawlings

IVY PRESS

First published in the UK in 2018 by
Ivy Press
An imprint of The Quarto Group
The Old Brewery, 6 Blundell Street
London N7 9BH, United Kingdom
T (0)20 7700 6700 **F** (0)20 7700 8066
www.QuartoKnows.com

Copyright © 2018 Quarto Publishing plc

All rights reserved. No part of this
book may be reproduced or
transmitted in any form by any means,
electronic or mechanical, including
photocopying, recording or by any
information storage-and-retrieval
system, without written permission
from the copyright holder.

British Library Cataloguing-in-
Publication Data
A catalogue record for this
book is available from the
British Library.

ISBN: 978-1-78240-554-2

This book was conceived,
designed and produced by
Ivy Press
58 West Street, Brighton BN1 2RA, UK

Publisher **Susan Kelly**
Creative Director **Michael Whitehead**
Editorial Director **Tom Kitch**
Senior Project Editor **Caroline Earle**
Designer **Ginny Zeal**
Illustrator **Steve Rawlings**
Picture Researcher **Sharon Dortenzio**
Glossaries Text **Mike Evans**

Cover images: Shutterstock/Inspiring: CL(BG);
Paper Wings: CR; sergey pozhoga: CL;
vectortatu: C(BG)

Typeset in Section

Printed in China

10 9 8 7 6 5 4 3 2 1

CITY AND COUNTY OF SWANSEA LIBRARIES	
6000330181	
Askews & Holts	09-Oct-2018
781.66	£14.99
SWOY	

CONTENTS

INTRODUCTION
Mike Evans

Rock music first emerged in the USA in the
mid-1950s as rock 'n' roll, and, spearheaded by million-selling records
by the likes of Elvis Presley and Little Richard, its popularity quickly
spread throughout the world. It was a musical and cultural explosion
the like of which had never been witnessed before.

Initially linked to the emergence of teenagers as a separate consumer
group in their own right, from the start rock was identified as music aimed
at, and purchased by, the young. Previous popular music, from romantic
crooners to swing-driven dance bands, certainly had its youthful audience,
but it was music shared with older generations – crucially, mum and dad
liked it too. Not so with rock, which throughout its history has managed
to shock or dumbfound parents, although ironically many of its leading
exponents and fans are now parents and grandparents themselves.

And although often being identified as the pop music of the day,
over the past 60-plus years rock has gone on to broaden its appeal in
a multitude of styles and genres, ranging from the solidly mainstream
to the boldly experimental.

The aim of this book is to provide a pocket-size history of rock music,
along with a brief guide to its various elements, while also tracing how
it has related to social trends and fashions, upon which it has often
exerted a significant influence.

How this book works
Beginning with **The Roots of Rock**, we trace the music's diverse origins,
from 1930s blues, gospel and hillbilly music, to the explosive 'birth of
the teenager' that shook the world in the early 1950s.

In **The Essence of Rock**, major genres – linked to specific periods in
rock's history – are outlined, from classic rock 'n' roll through prog rock,
heavy metal and punk, to today's indie and alt-rock.

How Rock Works describes the essential elements in the creation
of rock music, including the basic instrumentation, the historic part played

by vinyl singles and albums, the key role of producers and songwriters, and the live experience of touring bands playing everywhere from small clubs to massive arenas.

Rock's social influence is highlighted in the chapter on **Rock Culture**, tracing the music's impact on fashion, movies and literature, plus a look at the often-underrated role of women in rock music, and the function of rock as a voice of political dissent and protest.

Since its earliest days, from Buddy Holly and the Beatles, to Britpop and bubblegum records, **Rock as Pop** had been inextricably linked to the bestseller charts and idol-worshipping world of million-selling singles and fan mania.

Classic Records have been at the heart of rock music. It would be an impossible task to make a definitive list of a hundred, let alone just seven. But here are a selection of some of the very best spanning 60 years, evocative of their time as well as the music they represent.

Rock is truly an international music. In our run-down of cities in the **Rockin' Around the World** chapter, we've not gone for the historically most important – Liverpool, Memphis, New York and so on – but for a more arbitrary selection based both on past influence and a current cool connectivity.

Throughout the entries, records cited after a particular artist are usually their biggest, or most relevant, hit. Each entry is also accompanied by a 3-Second Lick summing up the topic, and 3-Minute Jam highlighting a particular aspect in more detail. All entries are followed by cross-referencing to related topics elsewhere in the book, and brief 3-Second Biographies of key individuals.

Finally, rock music has always been about its stars. Some of the most important names are featured in special Profile pieces, along with a brief timeline of their lives and careers, rounding off a compact guide to rock music that we hope will both inform and entertain at the same time.

A timeline of rock music

1948
Introduction of the vinyl long-player album

1949
RCA Records launch the 7-inch vinyl single

1951
Jackie Brenston's 'Rocket 88' released

1953
Marlon Brando stars as motorcycle gang leader in *The Wild One*. The Crows have first doo-wop chart hit with 'Gee'

1954
Elvis Presley's debut single 'That's All Right'. Bill Haley scores with his version of Joe Turner's rhythm and blues hit 'Shake, Rattle and Roll'

1955
James Dean teen-delinquent movie *Rebel Without a Cause* released. 'Rock Around the Clock' a huge hit for Bill Haley & His Comets

1956
Elvis's 'Heartbreak Hotel' tops charts

1958
First girl group hit, 'Maybe' by the Chantels

1959
Buddy Holly dies in plane crash

1960
The Miracles 'Shop Around' first big hit for Motown record company

1962
Beatles' debut single 'Love Me Do'

1963
The Freewheelin' Bob Dylan is released

1964
Beatles lead 'British Invasion' of USA

1965
Bob Dylan 'goes electric' at Newport Folk Festival. He releases *Bringing It All Back Home*

1966
Beach Boys' *Pet Sounds* released. Beatles' *Revolver* released

1967
Velvet Underground & Nico released. Beatles release *Sgt. Pepper's Lonely Hearts Club Band*. Monterey Pop Festival sets template for rock festivals to come

1968
Commercial debut of the Moog Synthesizer

1969
Woodstock Festival. *Led Zeppelin* debut album launches heavy rock. Rolling Stones guitarist Brian Jones dies

1970
Jimi Hendrix dies at 28. Beatles officially disband. Janis Joplin dies at 27. Jazz-rock chart breakthrough with Miles Davis's *Bitches Brew*

1972
David Bowie releases glam rock classic *The Rise and Fall of Ziggy Stardust*

1973
Progressive rock peaks
with Pink Floyd's *Dark
Side of the Moon*

1974
Kraftwerk's *Autobahn*
released. First punk acts
play CBGB club in New York

1976
Sex Pistols release punk
anthem 'Anarchy in the UK'

1977
Elvis Presley dies aged
42. Fleetwood Mac album
Rumours tops sales of
20 million

1978
Blondie release *Parallel
Lines*

1980
John Lennon murdered

1982
Compact discs introduced

1983
Yamaha launches DX-7,
the first mass-marketed
synthesizer

1984
Bruce Springsteen releases
'Born in the USA'

1985
'Live Aid' charity concert
televised worldwide

1989
'Madchester' scene in
Manchester, UK, leads with
Stone Roses' debut record

1991
Queen's Freddie Mercury
dies of AIDS

1992
Nirvana's *Nevermind*
tops US chart, launching
'grunge' music worldwide

1994
Nirvana vocalist Kurt
Cobain commits suicide

1995
Rock and Roll Hall of
Fame opens in Cleveland.
Britpop at its height, with
media-driven chart battle
between Blur and Oasis

1998
First portable MP3 player
introduced

1999
The White Stripes debut
album released

2001
George Harrison dies
aged 58

2003
Apple introduce 'iTunes'
online music service

2005
Guitar Hero video game
debuts on PlayStation 2

2006
Amy Winehouse releases
acclaimed album *Back to
Black*

2008
Spotify streaming service
launched

2014
Global digital music sales
surpass physical sales

2016
David Bowie dies

2017
Rock pioneers Chuck Berry
and Fats Domino die, aged
90 and 89 respectively

THE ROOTS OF ROCK

THE ROOTS OF ROCK
GLOSSARY

a cappella Unaccompanied singing, in early rock music usually associated with doo-wop vocal groups.

acoustic Pertaining to sound (as in the acoustic quality of a venue, for instance). More specifically, meaning unamplified, as in an acoustic non-electric guitar.

big band Precursors to the smaller line-ups of jump and early rhythm and blues bands, the big bands (typically featuring trumpets, trombones and saxophones fronting a piano-led rhythm section) were the most popular format for dance music and jazz through the 1930s and 1940s. The biggest names included Duke Ellington, Glenn Miller and Benny Goodman, but the blues-based 'Kansas City' sound of the Count Basie band and others was more directly influential as one of the ancestors of R&B and rock 'n' roll.

bluegrass Evolving from the music of the Appalachian Mountains, bluegrass has its roots in Irish, Scottish and English folk music, mixed with elements of blues and jazz. Its prime architect was Bill Monroe, and typically bluegrass is played on acoustic stringed instruments including the fiddle, banjo, guitar, mandolin and upright string bass. Additionally a resonator guitar (or Dobro) is often featured, as well as the occasional harmonica.

boogie-woogie A rhythmic piano style that evolved primarily in Chicago in the late 1920s, which features a left-hand 'walking bass' and is usually in the form of a 12-bar blues. Pioneers of the style included Pinetop Smith, but its most famous exponents during the boogie-woogie craze in the 1940s were Meade Lux Lewis and Albert Ammons. During the swing era the style was appropriated by many star names, including Tommy Dorsey and the Andrews Sisters.

bottleneck slides 'Slide' guitar playing involves moving an object up and down the strings to alter their pitch, rather than pressing down the strings with the fingers. This achieves the smooth transition from one note to the next that is a characteristic of blues music. Although slides can be bought commercially (usually small tubular metal objects that can be slipped onto the finger), country blues players often utilized a glass neck literally taken from a bottle – hence 'bottleneck', which also became the name of that particular style of blues playing.

call and response Where two vocal or instrumental phrases are played by two different musicians, the second in direct response to the first. Vocally, it was at the root of the field hollers and work songs that characterized much African-American music from the days of slavery, and the church-based gospel music that subsequently evolved in black communities across America.

chord progression A series of harmonies (or chords), also know as a chord sequence, that forms the underlying basis of a melody.

honky-tonk Guitar-based country-and-blues dance music, named after the 'honky-tonk' bars across the American Southwest, particularly Texas and Oklahoma, where it originated.

jump band Small-group rhythm and blues that followed the demise of the big swing bands after the Second World War, the style was most famously represented by 'King of the Jukebox' Louis Jordan.

juvenile delinquency A social scare in the early 1950s, particularly in the USA, as a newly affluent generation of 'teenagers' (as they were dubbed) flexed its muscles for the first time. Linked to the rise of rock 'n' roll, especially in films like *The Blackboard Jungle* and *Untamed Youth*.

pentatonic scales The simple five-note scale that forms the basis of much folk music, blues, gospel and jazz – and consequently rock music.

swing music The jazz dance-music style that predominated during the big band era of the 1930s and 1940s, with musicians like Benny Goodman and Artie Shaw the pop stars of their day.

COUNTRY BLUES

the 30-second rock

The blues are deeply rooted in the Mississippi Delta, the northwestern quarter of the state of Mississippi, an extremely fertile place for crops – and musicians. In the early 1900s, the region's vast plantations employed masses of black labourers, who had been enslaved only a generation earlier. The blues evolved from the call-and-response chants and 'field hollers' of these workers, and included a key development: the so-called 'blue notes', slightly flattened or sharpened for emotional emphasis. Country blues were songs of everyday trials, usually performed solo, with an acoustic guitar 'answering' the lyrics. Many of the most influential country blues performers hailed from the Delta: raspy-voiced Charley Patton, the soulful Son House and the mysterious guitar virtuoso Robert Johnson, although other key figures – Blind Lemon Jefferson (from Texas), Blind Willie McTell (Georgia) – hailed from elsewhere in the South. In the 1940s, better employment prospects drew bluesmen like Muddy Waters and Jimmy Reed north to Chicago, followed in the next decade by Howlin' Wolf, Elmore James and others. They brought with them the acoustic blues they had learned in the South, electrified it and played it in small combos. In the 1960s, these electric bluesmen inspired a host of British rockers.

3-SECOND LICK
Originating in the Deep South among black labourers, acoustic country blues became electrified in Chicago nightclubs and formed the bedrock of rock 'n' roll.

3-MINUTE JAM
The very foundation of rock guitar music is built upon the blues. Rock's basic chord progressions, the pentatonic scales for solos, its aggressively strummed chords, the bent notes, the use of bottleneck slides – all were pioneered by acoustic bluesmen like Charley Patton, Robert Johnson and Son House. Muddy Waters, raised on a plantation near Clarksdale, Mississippi, amplified House's slide guitar style and popularized it as the founding father of electric Chicago blues.

RELATED TOPICS
See also
RHYTHM & BLUES
page 18

CLASSIC ROCK 'N' ROLL
page 36

BEAT, BLUES & FOLK ROCK
page 38

3-SECOND BIOGRAPHIES
SON HOUSE
1902–88
Singer, slide guitarist, composer of 'Preachin' the Blues' and 'Death Letter'

ROBERT JOHNSON
1911–38
Singer, guitarist and composer of 'Cross Road Blues', 'Love in Vain' and 'Stop Breakin' Down Blues'

MUDDY WATERS
1913–83
Protégé of Son House, singer and popularizer of electric blues and slide guitar

30-SECOND TEXT
Paul Kingsbury

Born in rural Mississippi, country blues grew to influence rock's biggest stars.

RHYTHM & BLUES

the 30-second rock

3-SECOND LICK
From the honking saxes of 1940s jump bands to electric guitar blues, African-American rhythm and blues was the direct predecessor of rock 'n' roll.

3-MINUTE JAM
Big Joe Turner created the prototype for rhythm and blues when he banged out 'Roll 'Em Pete' in 1939, accompanied by the boogie-woogie pianist Pete Johnson. Nicknamed 'Boss of the Blues', in the early 1950s Turner had a string of R&B hits including 'Chains of Love' (1951), 'Honey Hush' (1953) and in 1954 the original version of 'Shake, Rattle and Roll' – which Bill Haley turned into a rock 'n' roll hit that same year.

The immediate progenitor of rock 'n' roll was rhythm and blues, which had its roots in the African-American 'jump' blues that flourished in the years following the Second World War. The term 'rhythm and blues' was coined in *Billboard* magazine in 1947, and in 1949 was used for what previously had been the 'race records' charts, of music primarily associated with the black community. The first big jump band star was Louis Jordan, who had a string of hits including 'Caldonia' (1945) and 'Choo Choo Ch'Boogie' (1946). Other early R&B hitmakers included Roy Milton ('RM Blues', 1946), Roy Brown ('Good Rockin' Tonight', 1947) and Joe Liggins ('Pink Champagne', 1950). Atlantic Records in New York was a pioneering R&B label, whose roster included Ruth Brown, Ray Charles and Big Joe Turner. Other prime movers in this genesis of rock music included Specialty Records in LA (with Lloyd Price, Jimmie Liggins and Little Richard), and Imperial, featuring the New Orleans stars Smiley Lewis and Fats Domino. And in Chicago, Chess Records promoted the electric blues of Muddy Waters, Howlin' Wolf and Little Walter, alongside proto-rockers Chuck Berry and Bo Diddley – not to mention the legendary 'first rock 'n' roll record', 'Rocket 88', in 1951.

RELATED TOPICS
See also
THE FIRST ROCK 'N' ROLL RECORD
page 28

CLASSIC ROCK 'N' ROLL
page 36

3-SECOND BIOGRAPHIES
LOUIS JORDAN
1908–75
Saxophonist and singer, had dozens of R&B hits between 1942 and 1950, nicknamed 'King of the Juke Box'

JERRY WEXLER
1917–2008
Key Atlantic Records producer, coined the term 'rhythm and blues' while at *Billboard* magazine in the late 1940s

RAY CHARLES
1930–2004
His unique blend of R&B and gospel ('What'd I Say', 1959) heralded 1960s soul music

30-SECOND TEXT
Mike Evans

R&B artists like Ray Charles, Chuck Berry and Louis Jordan forged the link between jazz, blues and rock music.

HILLBILLY TO ROCKABILLY

the 30-second rock

The first hillbilly superstar was Jimmie Rodgers, whose 1930s hits like 'Blue Yodel' fused folk, gospel and blues, selling millions of records. Country music came closer to jazz and swing in the 1940s with western swing, a fusion of the hillbilly guitar-and-fiddle sound and big band swing. Indeed, Bill Haley led a western swing outfit called the Saddlemen who cut one of rock's earliest records in 1952, 'Rock the Joint', before they were renamed the Comets and conquered the world with 'Rock Around the Clock'. Another branch of country music was known as hillbilly boogie; hits included the Delmore Brothers' 'Freight Train Boogie' in 1946, one of several titles later cited as the 'first rock 'n' roll record'. Honky-tonk music, a guitar-based style originating in Texas and Oklahoma, had its roots in western swing, the 'ranchera' music of the Tex-Mex border and Mississippi blues. So-named after the 'honky-tonk' bars where the potent dance music was played, early stars included Ernest Tubb and Kitty Wells. But the biggest name in honky-tonk was Hank Williams, with 30 top ten singles including 11 chart toppers. Bluegrass, a branch of country music steeped in the folk traditions of the Appalachian Mountains, was a huge influence on early country-flavoured rock music – 'rockabilly' – via its main architect, Bill Monroe.

RELATED TOPICS
See also
ELVIS PRESLEY
page 26

CLASSIC ROCK 'N' ROLL
page 36

3-SECOND BIOGRAPHIES
BILL MONROE
1911–96
Mandolin player, vocalist and songwriter who founded bluegrass music

HANK WILLIAMS
1923–53
Honky-tonk hero and country music's most revered superstar

BILL HALEY
1925–81
Recorded rock's original anthem 'Rock Around the Clock'

30-SECOND TEXT
Mike Evans

3-SECOND LICK
With its roots in European folk music and the blues of black America, hillbilly – later dubbed country music – was a prime ingredient in early rock.

3-MINUTE JAM
When the young Elvis Presley cut his first sides for Sun Records in Memphis in 1954, he chose Bill Monroe's 'Blue Moon of Kentucky' as the flipside of his debut disc 'That's All Right'. And it was this new breed of country-influenced rockers, including Elvis, Carl Perkins, Johnny Cash and Jerry Lee Lewis, that established 'rockabilly' as one of the key sounds in the birth of rock 'n' roll.

Honky-tonk heroes like Ernest Tubb (left) paved the way for the earliest rock 'n' roll stars such as Bill Haley (right).

GOSPEL & DOO-WOP

the 30-second rock

Slavery was abolished in the USA in 1865, but inequality for African-Americans remained a fact of life, especially in the South. Black communities sought solace in their churches, leading to the evolution of an uninhibited gospel music by the early twentieth century. Believing in 'good news in bad times', in 1932 Thomas A. Dorsey founded the first publishing company for black gospel music, and wrote 'Take My Hand, Precious Lord' and 'Peace in the Valley'. In the 1950s and early 1960s, church singers Sam Cooke and Aretha Franklin were criticized for switching to pop, and Ray Charles was censured for adapting gospel songs as rhythm and blues. Eventually the furore subsided, with gospel-rock crossovers becoming more commonplace. Vocal group doo-wop came out of gospel, with wordless syllables (hence the name) being sung behind the lead vocalist. The a cappella groups characteristically practised on street corners, and the Crows' 'Gee' (1953) is sometimes cited as the first rock 'n' roll record. The first international doo-wop hits were 'Only You' by The Platters (1955) and Frankie Lymon and The Teenagers' 'Why Do Fools Fall in Love' (1956). Doo-wop was not an exclusively black genre, with important participation by Italian-Americans from New York City, notably Dion and the Belmonts.

3-SECOND LICK
Religious fervour among African-Americans found its outlet in gospel music, with its call-and-response vocals subsequently inspiring doo-wop in major American cities during the 1950s.

3-MINUTE JAM
A significant proportion of the soul and soul-influenced performers of the 1960s acquired their skills from singing gospel music, and they brought these church-inspired techniques into their new genre. In addition, as Ray Charles and others demonstrated, there were many great gospel songs that could easily be adapted for new audiences. Similarly, the vocal techniques of the gospel singers were taken up by street-corner a capella doo-wop groups in New York, Philadelphia, Chicago and elsewhere.

RELATED TOPICS
See also
COUNTRY BLUES
page 16

ELVIS PRESLEY
page 26

GIRL GROUPS
page 98

MOTOWN
page 100

3-SECOND BIOGRAPHIES
SISTER ROSETTA THARPE
1915–73
Powerful gospel singer usually backed by her own electric guitar

FRANKIE LYMON
1942–68
A doo-wop star at 14 fronting Frankie Lymon and The Teenagers, but dead at 26

DION
1939–
Brought his voice and streetwise attitude to white doo-wop

30-SECOND TEXT
Spencer Leigh

Sister Rosetta Tharpe, and Rev. Thomas A. Dorsey were influential gospel personalities.

PRE-ROCK POP
the 30-second rock

In the pre-rock charts, the records were safe and unthreatening. A sure-fire way to a hit was a film theme, such as 'The Ballad of Davy Crockett' or 'Three Coins in the Fountain'. There were love songs ('Secret Love', 'Stranger in Paradise'), mushy religious ballads ('I Believe', 'Answer Me'), cheerful instrumentals ('Swedish Rhapsody', 'Cherry Pink and Apple Blossom White') and hundreds of novelties ('Poppa Piccolino', 'She Wears Red Feathers'). Most are all but forgotten, although some have endured such as Dean Martin's 'That's Amore' and Nat King Cole's 'Unforgettable'. Overall, the records were immaculately sung and performed, but usually lacked passion. Teenagers didn't want to hear songs eulogizing their fathers ('Oh Mein Papa') or the delights of their street ('Friends and Neighbours'). The first winds of change came in the early 1950s, from African-American rhythm and blues, and the highly emotional vocalist Johnnie Ray. Many vintage songs were reworked as rock 'n' roll, with The Platters' 'Smoke Gets in Your Eyes' (1958) being one of the finest examples. Veteran composer Irving Berlin chastised Elvis Presley for messing with 'White Christmas', while Richard Rodgers similarly disliked The Marcels' doo-wop treatment of 'Blue Moon', but they still banked the royalty cheques.

3-SECOND LICK
There was little to criticize in pre-rock pop, but little to praise either. Performers played safe, and songs were inoffensive. Memories aren't made of this.

3-MINUTE JAM
Following the Second World War, much of the popular music of the day was seen as escapism: pleasant sounds to make you forget the hardships around you, often glowing with kitsch religious sentiment. The talented performers rarely experimented, and the most inventive records of the period were often comedy items or children's novelties. There was nothing to excite teenagers (which in itself was a new word); that would have to wait until 1955.

RELATED TOPICS
See also
THE FIRST ROCK 'N' ROLL RECORD
page 28

THE BIRTH OF THE TEENAGER
page 30

BASIC INSTRUMENTATION
page 56

THE SINGLE
page 58

3-SECOND BIOGRAPHIES
IRVING BERLIN
1888–1989
The father of American popular song, never accepted rock 'n' roll

FRANK SINATRA
1915–98
Known, correctly, as The Voice

JOHNNIE RAY
1927–90
A not-so-easy listening singer, dubbed the 'Cry Guy' due to his on-stage histrionics

30-SECOND TEXT
Spencer Leigh

No ripped jeans or back-to-front baseball caps for Frank Sinatra and Nat King Cole.

8 January 1935
Born in Tupelo,
Mississippi, USA

1954
First recordings for Sun
Records in Memphis,
Tennessee

1955
RCA Records buys
his contract from Sun
Records for $35,000,
plus a $5,000 signing
bonus paid to Elvis

1956
Scores number one
hit US singles with
'Heartbreak Hotel',
'I Want You, I Need You,
I Love You', 'Don't Be
Cruel', 'Hound Dog' and
'Love Me Tender' and
just misses at number
two with 'Love Me'

1958
Joins the US Army for a
two-year tour of duty

1968
His hour-long comeback
special, *Elvis*, is televised
in the USA. It was the
most-watched US
television show that year

1969
Scores three top ten US
hits: 'In the Ghetto',
'Suspicious Minds' and
'Don't Cry Daddy'

16 August 1977
Dies at his home,
Graceland, in Memphis

ELVIS PRESLEY

Next to the Beatles, Elvis Presley is the most important act in rock history. He transformed rock 'n' roll from an obscure offshoot of rhythm and blues into the most popular music in the world. As John Lennon put it, 'Before Elvis, there was nothing'.

Elvis grew up in near poverty in the Mississippi Delta, the wellspring of the blues, and later in Memphis, Tennessee. He soaked up musical inspiration – from blues, country music, gospel and even crooner Dean Martin – and fused those seemingly disparate elements into an explosive mixture. In his earliest recordings, for Memphis's Sun Records beginning in 1954, he coupled the down-home feel of country music with the driving rhythm and cool of the blues, shaping 'rockabilly'.

Initially the music industry viewed him as strictly a country music performer. But as each single release outstripped the last in sales, and as his live performances drew increasingly frenzied crowds, he ended up in a bidding war among record labels vying to buy his contract from Sun. RCA Records prevailed, and in January 1956 released his landmark single 'Heartbreak Hotel'. It topped the US pop and country charts, and was a runaway bestseller – as was virtually everything he released for the next three years.

Elvis injected his songs with a powerful rhythmic energy and blues-inspired vocal gymnastics, ranging from rumbling low tones to falsetto coos and hiccups. On stage, he moved with a palpable sexuality that earned him the nickname 'Elvis the Pelvis', captivating young women and horrifying their parents. He also stirred hundreds of young men – including Buddy Holly, Carl Perkins, Roy Orbison and John Lennon – to pick up the beat and imitate him.

Following army service, Elvis recorded two of his best-loved hits in 1960: 'It's Now or Never' and 'Are You Lonesome Tonight?'. However, success sapped his ambition. For most of the 1960s he was content to record dull songs and star in a series of mediocre, low-budget movie musicals that blunted his artistic edge.

He mounted a comeback with a well-received December 1968 TV special, and in 1969 recorded fresh singles in Memphis that included the number one US hit 'Suspicious Minds'.

His last big chart hit was 'Burning Love' in 1972. Though he continued to record and tour, Elvis seemed largely irrelevant in the 1970s as rock moved on. He died at home in 1977, of an apparent heart attack brought on by prescription drug abuse.

Paul Kingsbury

THE FIRST ROCK 'N' ROLL RECORD

the 30-second rock

While the question of the first rock record has divided fans and critics over the years, the most frequently nominated for the place in the history books is a 1951 hit by Jackie Brenston and His Delta Cats, titled 'Rocket 88'. Brenston was a saxophone player and singer with Ike Turner's Kings of Rhythm, who in March 1951 cut four sides in Sam Phillips' still-to-be-famous recording studio in Memphis, Tennessee. Phillips would strike gold in 1954 when he recorded the 19-year-old Elvis for his Sun label, but back in 1951 Sam leased his recordings to other labels, and the songs recorded that day ended up with Chess Records of Chicago. Two sides sung by Turner were released as the Kings of Rhythm, while the two fronted by Brenston carried the sax man's moniker. An accident on the way to the session resulted in the guitar amp producing a fuzzy, distorted sound, which suited the number perfectly. The song, which was inspired by a car advertisement for the Oldsmobile 88 depicting a man and woman astride a spaceship 'riding the Rocket 88', was a huge hit with African-American record buyers, topping the national rhythm and blues chart in June 1951.

3-SECOND LICK
With its booting sax, and a broken amp distorting the guitar sound, 'Rocket 88' anticipated the sound of rock way ahead of its time.

3-MINUTE JAM
There have been various contenders for the title of the first rock 'n' roll record. Elvis Presley's debut 'That's All Right' from 1954 is often quoted as rock's earliest offspring, but for the first genuine rock 'n' roll record we have to look further back than that. One classic cited as rock's debut disc is 'The Fat Man', recorded by Fats Domino in 1949, with another strong candidate being Bill Haley's 'Rock the Joint' from 1952.

RELATED TOPICS
See also
RHYTHM & BLUES
page 18

CLASSIC ROCK 'N' ROLL
page 36

BASIC INSTRUMENTATION
page 56

THE SINGLE
page 58

3-SECOND BIOGRAPHIES
SAM PHILLIPS
1923–2003
Pioneering record producer and founder of Sun Records

JACKIE BRENSTON
1930–79
Vocalist and sax player on single 'Rocket 88'

IKE TURNER
1931–2007
R&B vocalist and bandleader, famous for work in the 1960s and 1970s with his wife Tina

30-SECOND TEXT
Mike Evans

Jackie Brenston and the Oldsmobile advert that inspired the title for his one and only hit.

THE BIRTH OF THE TEENAGER

the 30-second rock

RELATED TOPICS
See also
PRE-ROCK POP
page 24

ELVIS PRESLEY
page 26

CLASSIC ROCK 'N' ROLL
page 36

THE SINGLE
page 58

3-SECOND LICK
In the 1950s 'teenagers' were identified as a consumer group in their own right, and the music business responded with a new sound – rock 'n' roll.

3-MINUTE JAM
In the affluent USA of the 1950s, three out of four families considered themselves middle class, and had the house, car and TV set to prove it. Teenagers had their own portable record players for the new 7-inch singles, as well as mini transistor radios introduced in 1954. In many families, they also had the use of the 'second' car. And with the birth of rock 'n' roll, they had their own music as well.

Although it came into popular use in the early 1950s, the term 'teenager' was being used as early as the mid-1940s. In December 1944, for instance, *Life* magazine ran an article entitled 'Teen-Age Girls: They Live in a Wonderful World of Their Own'. The word was used more regularly from the early 1950s, as post-war America (and to a lesser degree Europe) enjoyed an unprecedented affluence, with a new generation of young people having money to spend on fashion, recreation and – most crucially – music. It was no coincidence, therefore, that the advent of rock 'n' roll came soon after the birth of the teenager. Two movies spotlighted the new youth culture – *The Wild One* (1953) with Marlon Brando leading a motorcycle gang, and James Dean's sensational teen-angst drama *Rebel Without a Cause* (1955). Notably, neither film's soundtrack featured a note of rock music – had either been made in 1956 or later, it would have been a different story. Both movies focused on the much-publicized 'problem' of juvenile delinquency, which, despite some sensational press coverage, was not the threat to civilization many feared. 'I'm Not a Juvenile Delinquent' sang 14-year-old Frankie Lymon in 1956, on one of the first doo-wop songs to hit the charts; his backing group, significantly, were called The Teenagers.

3-SECOND BIOGRAPHIES
MARLON BRANDO
1924–2004
Classic 'method' actor, in *The Wild One* he personified teenage delinquency though aged nearly 30 at the time

JAMES DEAN
1931–55
Immortalized the archetypal troubled teenager as Jim Stark in *Rebel Without a Cause*

30-SECOND TEXT
Mike Evans

Marlon Brando, alongside music idols like Elvis, was just one of the pin-ups that adorned teenagers' bedroom walls in the 1950s.

THE ESSENCE OF ROCK

THE ESSENCE OF ROCK
GLOSSARY

beat poetry The 'beat generation' writers of the mid-1950s, most famously Allen Ginsberg (*Howl*, 1956) and Jack Kerouac (*On the Road*, 1957), inspired a free-form 'stream of consciousness' style of lyric writing in the work of a number of rock songwriters including Bob Dylan, John Lennon and Tom Waits.

boogie-woogie A rhythmic piano style that evolved primarily in Chicago in the late 1920s, which features a left-hand 'walking bass' and is usually in the form of a 12-bar blues. Pioneers of the style included Pinetop Smith, but its most famous exponents during the boogie-woogie craze in the 1940s were Meade Lux Lewis and Albert Ammons. During the swing era the style was appropriated by many star names, including Tommy Dorsey and the Andrews Sisters.

British Invasion Journalistic term for the huge assault of UK artists on the US charts in the wake of the Beatles, and subsequent 'invasion' of live touring bands. Major names included the Rolling Stones, the Dave Clark Five and Herman's Hermits, as well as solo names such as Tom Jones, Petula Clark and Donovan. In June 1965, no fewer than 14 British records occupied the US top forty. A big influence on US guitar-led groups of the mid-1960s, including the Beach Boys, Lovin' Spoonful and the Byrds.

concept album An album with a common theme or storyline throughout. Although thematic albums were not new, the Beatles' *Sgt. Pepper* is acknowledged as establishing the fashion in rock music, with the format coming into its own in the early 1970s with the grandiose ambitions of progressive rock.

grunge Specifically describing the alternative rock of 1990s (mainly) Seattle bands including Nirvana, Soundgarden and Pearl Jam, and similar groups who followed in their wake.

long-player (LP) Launched in 1948, the long-playing vinyl album running at 33 revolutions per minute (rpm) revolutionized popular music, ending the time restraints of the three-minute single. Usually in a 12-inch format, LPs also generated album artwork, some of which became as iconic as the music itself.

Mellotron An electronic keyboard launched in England in the 1960s, that used tape-recorded replay to achieve a variety of effects.

Merseybeat A catch-all term for bands that came out of Liverpool immediately after the UK success of the Beatles in 1963, the typical line-up consisted of two guitars, bass guitar and drums. The repertoire of most groups was classic and early-1960s US rock 'n' roll and R&B, with leading exponents including the Searchers, Gerry & the Pacemakers and the Swinging Blue Jeans.

Moog synthesizer Named after designer Robert Moog, a generic name for analog music synthesizers that revolutionized electronic music in the late 1960s, an advance on the tape-recorded effects of the Mellotron.

psychedelic Pertaining to the effects of hallucinogenic drugs (primarily LSD), and describing music, art and literature inspired by their use.

riff Originating in jazz, referring to a repeated instrumental phrase that identifies a song or provides a backing link – or indeed both.

skiffle A do-it-yourself UK music craze in the 1950s, with a typical home-made group featuring guitars and a 'rhythm section' of washboard and tea-chest bass. Popularized by Lonnie Donegan after his 1955 hit 'Rock Island Line', skiffle had its roots in the American 'jug bands' of the 1920s. As well as introducing a generation of British fans to authentic blues and folk music, the movement was a breeding ground for rock musicians of the 1960s, with the Beatles, Jimmy Page and many more having their beginnings in skiffle.

three-chord rock Straightforward rock based on the three basic chords of the 12-bar blues.

whammy bar Control lever on an electric guitar, used to add vibrato to the sound by changing the tension of the strings.

CLASSIC ROCK 'N' ROLL
the 30-second rock

The classic sound of rock 'n' roll first appeared in the charts in 1955, with hits featuring the boogie-based style of Bill Haley & His Comets ('Rock Around the Clock' and five more), and the New Orleans rhythm and blues of Fats Domino ('Ain't That a Shame'). Then early in 1956, with the million-selling 'Heartbreak Hotel', Elvis Presley's bluesy sound added some down-home spice to the mix. From then on, through the latter half of the 1950s, the charts were increasingly dominated by rock 'n' roll records aimed at a predominantly teenage market. Some were clearly in the successful Presley mould, such as Gene Vincent's 'Be-Bop-A-Lula' (1956). Jerry Lee Lewis ('Great Balls of Fire', 1957) on the other hand, combined the raw rockabilly of early Elvis with the piano-pumping, gospel-inspired shout of Little Richard ('Long Tall Sally', 1956). Buddy Holly ('That'll Be the Day', 1957) and the Everly Brothers ('Wake Up Little Susie', 1957) brought a Southern sound of their own to the charts, while black R&B continued to permeate the mainstream with hits by the likes of Chuck Berry ('Sweet Little Sixteen', 1958), the Coasters ('Yakety Yak', 1958) and Larry Williams ('Short Fat Fannie', 1957).

3-SECOND LICK
Classic rock 'n' roll has been a key influence on generations of musicians, from the Beatles and the Rolling Stones, to Elvis Costello and The White Stripes.

3-MINUTE JAM
Disc jockey Alan Freed (1921–65) was a key figure in the popularization of rock 'n' roll – and the first to use the term widely – in the early to mid-1950s, with his pioneering radio shows, live package tours and appearances in movies like *Rock Around the Clock* (1956) and *Mr Rock and Roll* (1957). He died in penury in 1965, after his career was ruined by the 'payola' scandal, involving record company hand-outs to DJs in return for plugging certain records.

RELATED TOPICS
See also
THE FIRST ROCK 'N' ROLL RECORD
page 28

ELVIS PRESLEY: 'HEARTBREAK HOTEL'
page 116

3-SECOND BIOGRAPHIES
FATS DOMINO
1928–2017
New Orleans pianist-vocalist, with more than 20 US top 30 hits between 1954 and 1960

LITTLE RICHARD
1932–
'Tutti Frutti' (1955) with its opening line 'A-wop-bop-a-loo-bop-a-wop-bam-boom!' heralded rock 'n' roll

BUDDY HOLLY
1936–59
His death in 1959 in a plane crash signalled, for many, 'the day the music died'

30-SECOND TEXT
Mike Evans

The Everly Brothers, Fats Domino and Chuck Berry dominated jukeboxes worldwide.

PRESS A
LETTER-BUTTON
AND A
NUMBER-BUTTON
FOR EACH
SELECTION

A B C D E F G H J K
1 2 3 4 5 6 7 8 9 10

MAKE SELECTION
AFTER
DEPOSITING
EACH
COIN

BEAT, BLUES & FOLK ROCK

the 30-second rock

3-SECOND LICK
When Bob Dylan famously 'went electric' at the 1965 Newport Folk Festival, it marked a point where rock music was being regarded 'seriously' for the first time.

3-MINUTE JAM
The British 'beat boom' spearheaded by the Beatles and the Rolling Stones, reminded American teenagers of their own country's rich musical heritage, from the blues of Robert Johnson to the rock 'n' roll of Chuck Berry. And as a side-product of the American folk music revival – drawing on a mix of 1940s political songs, 1950s beat poetry, traditional blues and the new beat music from Great Britain – a new genre was forged, which the critics called folk rock.

With Elvis in the army, Buddy

Holly dead and Chuck Berry in jail, the late 1950s to early 1960s marked a low point for American rock 'n' roll, with a succession of bland imitators holding sway. But the 1964 British Invasion, led by the Beatles, alerted American audiences to their own musical heritage. Groups like the Rolling Stones and the Animals demonstrated the influence of the blues and R&B in their music, reviving the careers of veterans like Howlin' Wolf and Sonny Boy Williamson in the process. Meanwhile a new wave of home-grown US talent including Bob Dylan, Joan Baez and Tom Paxton was at the forefront of a folk music revival, inspired by the 'protest' heritage of Woody Guthrie and others from the 1940s. The Newport Folk Festivals of 1963 to 1965 provided a platform for long-forgotten bluesmen like Mississippi John Hurt, Muddy Waters and John Lee Hooker, sharing stages with young enthusiasts such as Dylan, Baez, and Peter, Paul & Mary. And the 1950s 'Beat Generation' writers – Jack Kerouac, Allen Ginsberg and so on – were also a big influence on Dylan's drug-inspired lyrics of the mid-1960s, anticipating the 'psychedelic' music of bands like the Grateful Dead and Jefferson Airplane later in the decade.

RELATED TOPICS
See also
CLASSIC ROCK 'N' ROLL
page 36

THE BEATLES
page 40

THE ROLLING STONES
page 64

BOB DYLAN
page 86

3-SECOND BIOGRAPHIES
JOHN LEE HOOKER
1917–2001
Veteran bluesman whose career was revived by the 'blues boom' in the 1960s

JOAN BAEZ
1941–
American folk singer at the forefront of the 1960s folk revival

30-SECOND TEXT
Patrick Humphries

Folk queen Joan Baez looms over Peter, Paul & Mary in concert; folk revival godfather Woody Guthrie; and new boys the Rolling Stones.

1957
John Lennon's skiffle group, the Quarrymen, play the Cavern club in Liverpool

1958
The Quarrymen make a private recording

1960
John, Paul, George Harrison, Stuart Sutcliffe and Pete Best – the Beatles – perform among Hamburg's strip clubs

1962
John, Paul, George and Ringo record their first single for Parlophone

1963
With fellow performers, 'Merseybeat' sweeps the UK charts

1964
A record audience of 73 million Americans watch the Beatles on *The Ed Sullivan Show*

1965
The Beatles receive MBEs from the Queen, and release 'Yesterday', the most recorded song of all time

1966
US controversy as Lennon says the Beatles are more popular than Jesus. *Revolver* continues that popularity, but the group play their final concert in San Francisco

1967
Release of experimental 'Strawberry Fields Forever', and *Sgt. Pepper's Lonely Hearts Club Band*

1968
The Beatles (aka 'The White Album'), a double album of songs written mostly in India

1969
The Beatles make their last-ever live appearance, on the rooftop of their London offices

1970
The group breaks up officially, as Paul McCartney files a suit against his former bandmates

THE BEATLES

The Beatles started inauspiciously as an acoustic skiffle group, the Quarrymen, at a garden fete in the Woolton suburb of Liverpool in July 1957, where the leader John Lennon (1940–80) met Paul McCartney (1942–). Subsequently McCartney's schoolfriend, George Harrison (1943–2001), an impressive young guitarist, joined – and referencing Buddy Holly's Crickets, they became the Beatles. With John's art school companion Stuart Sutcliffe on bass guitar, and drummer Pete Best, they went to Hamburg in August 1960 for the first of five residencies. Astrid Kirchherr took unforgettable photographs, Jürgen Vollmer suggested mop-top haircuts, and the Beatles' 'look' was born. Sutcliffe left the group to study art, but died from a brain aneurysm in 1962.

The group developed a raw, raucous sound based around American rock 'n' roll, and gained a teenage following both in Hamburg and Liverpool. Brian Epstein became their manager, and in August 1962 he replaced Best with Ringo Starr (1940–). Signing with EMI's Parlophone label, they scored modestly with 'Love Me Do' in October 1962, followed by a series of up-tempo, chart-topping UK singles all written by Lennon and McCartney. 'Beatlemania' spread to America in 1964, with appearances on The Ed Sullivan Show and increasingly chaotic arena concerts, most famously at New York's Shea Stadium in 1965. They satirized their success in the movie A Hard Day's Night (1964) with wit and panache, but the follow-up Help! (1965) was hampered by a puerile plot.

Encouraged by producer George Martin, their recordings became increasingly inventive, with the ground-breaking Revolver (1966) and Sgt. Pepper's Lonely Hearts Club Band (1967). Advances in technology added depth to their sound, and they broke rules simply because they didn't know what the rules were. The classical-sounding 'Eleanor Rigby' has been compared to Schubert, but this was never McCartney's intention.

Epstein died in 1967, and although consoled by the meditation guru Maharishi Mahesh Yogi, the Beatles were comparatively rudderless through Magical Mystery Tour and the so-called 'White Album'. The sessions filmed for the Let It Be documentary showed their inner turmoil, but they returned to top form for their last-recorded album, Abbey Road (1969).

Their solo careers were impressive, and the world was shocked by the assassination of John Lennon in 1980. Their legacy continues with Broadway and West End plays, films, Beatlefests, McCartney's live concerts and the acknowledgement of almost every successful musician. No other act has matched their worldwide critical acclaim and popular success, and they remain an essential component in the development of popular music.

Spencer Leigh

PROGRESSIVE ROCK

the 30-second rock

3-SECOND LICK
Despite many critics'
efforts, 'prog' rock
endures, testified by the
longevity of Pink Floyd
and Genesis. Reunions,
box sets, magazines and
autobiographies ensure
prog's continued
popularity.

3-MINUTE JAM
Characterized by complex
and ornate styles of rock
music popularized in the
1970s, progressive rock
encouraged instrumental
virtuosity and conceptual
themes on a grand scale.
Elaborate cover art,
'meaningful' lyrics and
musical experimentation
flourished during the high
watermark of the genre.
Although initially thought
to have been obliterated by
punk, indie rock and such,
prog rock endured with
Marillion in the 1980s,
and bands like Porcupine
Tree on into the twenty-
first century.

If any one LP marked the
beginning of progressive rock, it was surely
the Beatles' *Sgt. Pepper's Lonely Hearts Club
Band* (1967). The first album to feature lyrics on
its sleeve, and the first to lose the gaps between
tracks, it tested Abbey Road Studios capabilities
to the limit. Groups such as Pink Floyd flexed
rock's boundaries further, with albums such as
A Saucerful of Secrets (1968). By the end of
the 1960s, 'pop' had become 'rock', with album
sales overtaking singles. Emerson, Lake &
Palmer and Deep Purple embraced classical
elements, and The Who's *Tommy* (1969) was
marketed as 'a rock opera'. King Crimson's *In
the Court of the Crimson King* (1969) featured
extensive use of the Mellotron, while the Moog
synthesizer was soon ubiquitous. By the middle
of the 1970s, Yes had felt confident enough to
issue a triple live LP and a double concept
album, *Tales from Topographic Oceans* (1973).
Spectacular sleeve designs by Storm Thorgerson
and Roger Dean were key to prog's success.
In 1976, punk was a wilful response to the
excesses of prog, with the likes of the Sex
Pistols and Ramones finding drum solos,
pretentious lyrics and concept albums
increasingly redundant. However, against
expectations, the genre has survived and
progressed into the twenty-first century.

RELATED TOPICS
See also
ELECTRO-ROCK
page 48

THE ALBUM
page 60

PRODUCERS
page 62

KEY CROSSOVERS
page 88

3-SECOND BIOGRAPHIES
ROGER WATERS
1943–
Singer, songwriter, bass player
and co-founder of Pink Floyd

RICK WAKEMAN
1949–
Keyboardist with David Bowie,
the Strawbs and Yes

PHIL COLLINS
1951–
Singer-songwriter and drummer
with Genesis. Later enjoyed
huge success as a solo artist

30-SECOND TEXT
Patrick Humphries

*Peter Gabriel in excelsis
on stage with Genesis;
Yes relax after sailing
Topographic Oceans.*

HEAVY METAL

the 30-second rock

No one knows for certain how the term 'heavy metal' came to be applied to aggressive, heavily amplified rock. But it was a fitting label for the hard guitar crunch pioneered by British acts like The Who and the Jeff Beck Group in the late 1960s. In its first flowering, heavy metal was much influenced by the blues. Leading lights included Eric Clapton with his band Cream, Jimi Hendrix and Led Zeppelin, who balanced their blues thunder with acoustic folk and Celtic touches. Black Sabbath reset the course for heavy metal in the 1970s; eschewing the blues, Sabbath focused on sledgehammer riff interplay among guitar, bass and drums, and doom-laden wailing from Ozzy Osbourne. In the 1980s, Iron Maiden and Judas Priest led the 'new wave of heavy metal' with chugging, lockstep twin guitars, howling vocals and ominous lyrics. With more melodic approaches, Def Leppard, Guns N' Roses and Van Halen showed metal could sell in the multi-millions. Eddie Van Halen advanced metal guitar, with his innovative fretboard tapping and whammy bar techniques. Emerging from the 1980s–1990s speed metal pack, which included Megadeth and Slayer, Metallica forged a pile-driving, ferocious sound tempered with a rhythmic and melodic sophistication that expanded their audience beyond the usual teenage head-bangers.

3-SECOND LICK
Characterized by distorted electric guitars, thunderous drums and harsh vocals, heavy metal retains a strong youth following even as it enters its sixth decade.

3-MINUTE JAM
Though heavy metal's original core is to be found in the classic sounds of Black Sabbath and Metallica, the genre has continued to evolve. In the 1990s and 2000s, 'nu metal' bands like Linkin Park, Limp Bizkit, Papa Roach and Korn emerged, melding the gut-punch of traditional metal with the wordplay, beats and samples of rap.

RELATED TOPICS
See also
THE BIRTH OF THE TEENAGER
page 30

BEAT, BLUES & FOLK ROCK
page 38

INDIE & ALT-ROCK
page 50

JIMI HENDRIX
page 124

3-SECOND BIOGRAPHIES
OZZY OSBOURNE
1948–
Lead vocalist of Black Sabbath (1969–79, 2012–13), solo vocalist and reality television star (*The Osbournes*, 2002–05)

EDDIE VAN HALEN
1955–
Leader and virtuoso guitarist of the band Van Halen

30-SECOND TEXT
Paul Kingsbury

Exploring the possibilities in aggressive sounds, heavy metal musicians have found release – and eager audiences – in cranking up the amps.

PUNK & NEW WAVE

the 30-second rock

3-SECOND LICK
Punk rock, and its more commercial relative, new wave, reinvented the original wild, untamed spirit of basic rock 'n' roll.

3-MINUTE JAM
Punk and new wave are thought of as movements primarily centred in the USA and the UK, but Australia made its contribution too. The Saints' single '(I'm) Stranded' was one of the first punk records released outside America, and Radio Birdman were considered equally seminal. As far as the new wave was concerned, both Men at Work and Midnight Oil were among the Australian bands who achieved international success.

In the USA, punk sprang from the scene that developed around the New York City club CBGB in 1974, where acts like Television, Patti Smith and the Ramones stripped rock 'n' roll back to its three-chord basics. Punk was also a look; long hair and flared trousers were replaced by close-cropped haircuts and straight-legged jeans. A cross-pollination with London began with Malcolm McLaren, a Londoner in New York managing proto-punk act the New York Dolls, who was fascinated by the sound and the look of the emerging music scene. On returning to London after the New York Dolls broke up, he began managing the group that became the standard-bearers of punk: the Sex Pistols. The Pistols outraged the public with their nihilistic antics and anti-establishment songs like 'God Save the Queen' (1977), and bands like The Clash and The Damned followed in their wake. The rebellious stance of the bands didn't keep them from signing with major labels, however. But the big record companies were more comfortable dealing with so-called 'new wave' acts – bands who were equally energetic, but more pop-oriented and melodic than anarchic punk rockers. They would also be commercially successful; acts like Blondie, the Police, the Cars and Elvis Costello sold far more records than punk bands.

RELATED TOPICS
See also
INDIE & ALT-ROCK
page 50

BASIC INSTRUMENTATION
page 56

FOLLOWERS OF FASHION
page 76

REBEL REBEL: ROCK AS PROTEST MUSIC
page 84

3-SECOND BIOGRAPHIES
HILLY KRISTAL
1931–2007
Owner and booker of CBGB

MALCOLM MCLAREN
1946–2010
Manager of the Sex Pistols and Bow Wow Wow; designer, visual artist and performer

JOHNNY ROTTEN
1956–
Vocalist in the Sex Pistols, later in Public Image Ltd

30-SECOND TEXT
Gillian G. Gaar

In the 1970s, punk injected a welcome shot of energy into the music scene.

ELECTRO-ROCK

the 30-second rock

Electronic instruments were increasingly being used in the 1960s to enhance rock songs; the Beatles used a Mellotron on 'Strawberry Fields Forever' (1967) while The Monkees' *Pisces, Aquarius, Capricorn & Jones Ltd.* (1967) was one of the first rock albums to use a Moog synthesizer. By the end of the decade, electronic music began coming into its own; in 1969, Dick Hyman's 'The Minotaur' became the first Moog instrumental to reach the US top 40, while Hot Butter's 1972 electronic piece 'Popcorn' was a hit on both sides of the Atlantic. In the 1970s, Kraftwerk spearheaded the 'krautrock' movement of German bands who solely used electronic instruments (other key groups being Can, Faust and Tangerine Dream). Electro-rock, sometimes referred to as Synthpop, was especially popular in Europe; as it was generally devoid of lyrics, there was no language barrier to worry about. France's Jean-Michel Jarre achieved international fame with his 1976 album *Oxygène*; Jarre's style was based more on melody as opposed to the rhythmic pulse of other electronic music. Greek composer Evangelos Odysseas Papathanassiou – known as Vangelis – found fame with his electronic score for the 1981 film *Chariots of Fire*. Japanese musicians like Isao Tomika and Yellow Magic Orchestra also made notable contributions to the genre.

RELATED TOPICS
See also
PROGRESSIVE ROCK
page 42

DIGITAL ROCK – THE FUTURE?
page 90

BERLIN
page 144

TOKYO
page 152

3-SECOND BIOGRAPHIES
ROBERT ARTHUR MOOG
1934–2005
Inventor of the Moog

GIORGIO MORODER
1940–
Songwriter, producer of electronic music, soundtracks and disco hits

JEAN-MICHEL JARRE
1948–
French composer and musician, best known for *Oxygène*

30-SECOND TEXT
Gillian G. Gaar

Electro artists like Jean-Michel Jarre have found chart success, particularly in Europe.

3-SECOND LICK
Over the decades, numerous acts have shown that you don't need a guitar – or indeed bass or drums – to create imaginative rock music.

3-MINUTE JAM
In the late 1970s, Italian-born Giorgio Moroder emerged as a major force in electronic dance music. In 1977, Donna Summer's 'I Feel Love' (co-written by Moroder, Summer and Pete Bellotte, and co-produced by Moroder and Bellotte), set a new standard, with a completely synthesized backing track and hard beats instead of the melodic strings featured in other dance music of the era. Moroder's work with Summer in particular brought electronic music fully into the mainstream.

INDIE & ALT-ROCK
the 30-second rock

Nirvana's breakthrough success

in the early 1990s was seen by some as surprising and unexpected; but it was actually the result of the continued growth of the independent music scene, which had emerged in the 1980s. Fuelled by the iconoclastic energy of 1970s-era punk, indie bands eschewed commercialism in favour of creating music with a more distinctive, individualistic style, presenting themselves as an alternative to the pop mainstream (hence 'alt-rock'). Such bands were supported by a network of fanzines, independent record labels and college radio stations, and they played in 'alternative' venues such as art galleries and warehouses, as much as clubs. In the UK, The Smiths enjoyed chart success while on an independent label, but found it harder to crack the USA; neither Hüsker Dü or the Replacements found commercial success, despite being signed to major labels. Bands like R.E.M., Jane's Addiction and Sonic Youth paved the way for the 1990s grunge explosion that included Nirvana, Pearl Jam and Soundgarden. This opened further doors, as major labels were no longer as wary of the indie/alt-rock label, with acts like Green Day, Radiohead and Beck all finding success. After a post-grunge slump, the spirit of alt-rock has been kept alive by acts like The White Stripes, Arctic Monkeys, the Hives and the Vines.

RELATED TOPICS
See also
NIRVANA: *NEVERMIND*
page 128

THE WHITE STRIPES: *THE WHITE STRIPES*
page 130

SEATTLE
page 140

3-SECOND BIOGRAPHIES
BONO
1960–
Irish singer-songwriter, lead vocalist with U2

EDDIE VEDDER
1964–
Guitarist and lead vocalist with Seattle band Pearl Jam

KURT COBAIN
1967–94
Lead singer and founder of grunge pioneers Nirvana

30-SECOND TEXT
Gillian G. Gaar

3-SECOND LICK
A thriving independent rock scene has played a crucial role in injecting the mainstream with a regular jolt of creativity.

3-MINUTE JAM
Once indie rock bands found success, it set up a conundrum: could you really be 'alt-rock' if you had hit records? Some bands, like Nirvana and Green Day, reacted defensively, releasing records (*In Utero* and *Insomniac*, respectively) disparaging their new fame. But others, including the Red Hot Chili Peppers and U2, transitioned more readily, U2 in particular using their fame to promote various social causes they identified with.

Sonic Youth (above) paved the way for alt-rock acts like R.E.M. (below) to cross over into the mainstream.

HOW ROCK WORKS

HOW ROCK WORKS
GLOSSARY

British Invasion Journalistic term for the huge assault of UK artists on the US charts in the wake of the Beatles, and subsequent 'invasion' of live touring bands. Major names included the Rolling Stones, the Dave Clark Five and Herman's Hermits, as well as solo names such as Tom Jones, Petula Clark and Donovan. In June 1965, no fewer than 14 British records occupied the US top forty. A big influence on US guitar-led groups of the mid-1960s, including the Beach Boys, Lovin' Spoonful and the Byrds.

crooner Pre-rock male pop singer popular from the 1930s to 1950s, with a casual, jazz-influenced style personified by the two biggest names Bing Crosby and Frank Sinatra.

heritage act An established big-name rock act, whose career peaked as far back as the 1960s or 1970s, that still tours arena venues and festivals, largely relying on past glories to draw the crowds. Prime examples are Paul McCartney, Fleetwood Mac and the Rolling Stones.

jump band Small-group rhythm and blues that followed the demise of the big swing bands after the Second World War, the style was most famously represented by 'King of the Jukebox' Louis Jordan.

long-player (LP) Launched in 1948, the long-playing vinyl album running at 33 revolutions per minute (rpm) revolutionized popular music, ending the time restraints of the three-minute single. Usually in a 12-inch format, LPs also generated album artwork, some of which became as iconic as the music itself.

mono Or monaural. Sound recording using only one single channel, heard as if coming from a single position. The only system available until the advent of stereo recording in 1957.

psychedelic rock Pertaining to the effects of hallucinogenic drugs (primarily LSD), instrumental music and lyrics inspired by their use. Prime examples include albums by the Grateful Dead, Jefferson Airplane and the British pop-psychedelia of Pink Floyd's 'See Emily Play'.

rock opera A collection of songs related to a common theme or story, typically released as a concept album during the progressive rock period. Songs are not usually linked by an acted script, as opposed to traditional opera. The first major example of rock opera was 1969's *Tommy* by The Who.

sampling The technique of taking a section (sample) from one recording and reusing it in another piece. Originally used in experimental electronic music, later featured in psychedelic rock and jazz fusion; from the 1970s a major part of hip-hop music, with DJs sampling 'live' with the aid of two turntables and an audio mixer.

scratching DJ technique widely used in rap, hip-hop and related rock, of moving a vinyl record back and forth on a turntable to produce percussive sounds and effects, while manipulating the crossfader on an audio mixer.

stereo Or stereophonic. Two-channel recording, giving the impression of sound coming from left, middle and right. First introduced on commercial recordings by the American label Audio Fidelity in 1957.

studio album An album specifically recorded in a series of studio sessions, as opposed to a 'live' album recorded at an on-stage performance, or a compilation album of tracks from various periods and sources.

Tin Pan Alley Generic name for the traditional songwriting industry, before and during the rock era. Originally referred to a specific area of Manhattan in New York City, on West 28th Street, where most music publishers were based from the late nineteenth century. With the advent of rock 'n' roll, the centre shifted to the Brill Building on West 49th and Broadway. The name is said to come from a derogatory reference to the noise of many pianos playing simultaneously in the publishers' offices, comparing it to the banging of tin pans.

BASIC INSTRUMENTATION

the 30-second rock

3-SECOND LICK

Rock's core identity is in its beats. Regardless of how the instrumentation evolves – from drums and guitars to synth drums and computers – rhythm remains king.

3-MINUTE JAM

The electric guitar, developed by pioneers like Les Paul in the 1930s, epitomizes rock 'n' roll and gave the genre its original identity. However, there are few genuine rock songs that don't rely just as heavily on drums. Drummers (and, more recently, synth drum programmers) may often be hidden from the glare of the spotlight, but they are rock's vital heartbeat and its unsung heroes.

Driving beats distinguish rock from most other music genres. The dance-friendly jump-blues bands that presaged rock 'n' roll typically consisted of drums, string bass, piano, guitar and saxophone. But once Elvis Presley, Chuck Berry and Buddy Holly broke loose in the mid-1950s with a raw, new sound that blended blues with country music, the typical rock band was pared down to drums, string bass and two guitars. Because the Beatles and British Invasion bands revered those musicians, they duplicated such instrumentation, except for substituting the cheaper, easier-to-play electric bass guitar for string bass. Into the 1970s, most rock bands were guitar-focused, though keyboards became increasingly common. The synthesizer's commercial advent in 1968 was ground-breaking. It was quickly embraced, notably by the Beatles on *Abbey Road* (1969) and The Who on *Who's Next* (1971). Producer Giorgio Moroder broke barriers in 1977 with electronic drums and a completely synthesized backing track for Donna Summer's 'I Feel Love'. Emerging with Grandmaster Flash & the Furious Five's seminal hit 'Freedom' in 1980, the use of sampling by rappers rang yet another significant change. Subsequent leaps in digital technology now make it possible for musicians to play and record entirely on a laptop. And the beat goes on.

RELATED TOPICS

See also
RHYTHM & BLUES
page 18

PROGRESSIVE ROCK
page 42

ELECTRO-ROCK
page 48

3-SECOND BIOGRAPHIES

LES PAUL
1915–2009
Jazz, blues and country guitarist; a pioneer of the solid-bodied electric guitar, which made possible the basic sound of rock 'n' roll

GRANDMASTER FLASH
1958–
DJ and leader of Grandmaster Flash & the Furious Five, pioneers of scratching, sampling and culturally probing rap lyrics ('The Message', 1982)

30-SECOND TEXT
Paul Kingsbury

At its heart, the basic instrumentation of rock has always been about the beat.

THE SINGLE

the 30-second rock

A famous jazz musician once said, 'if you can't say it in three minutes, it's not worth saying' – or words to that effect. From its birth, rock music was defined by that same exercise in musical economy: keep it simple, keep it tight and, with a catchy chorus, you might have a hit on your hands. The first rock 'n' roll singles in 1955–6 were still the bulky 10-inch '78s' (78 rpm, or 78 revolutions per minute) made of highly breakable shellac. But it was when the virtually unbreakable 7-inch vinyl '45' came into its own that the pop single really took off. For the next ten years the history of rock was reflected in the singles charts – between 1956 and 1960, for instance, Elvis Presley sold over 35 million singles in America alone, while the Beatles shifted 23 million in the USA during the 1960s, complemented by increasingly huge album sales. And despite being overtaken by the album by the end of the decade, the single underwent a revival with the advent of punk in the late 1970s, and has remained a potent marker of success for alternative rock bands, mainstream artists and dance-oriented pop, be it in vinyl, CD or downloaded formats.

3-SECOND LICK
Ever since the invention of the domestic gramophone at the end of the nineteenth century, the three-minute single has defined popular music of all kinds.

3-MINUTE JAM
The role of the 7-inch '45' in the birth of rock 'n' roll cannot be overstated. The music of Little Richard, Buddy Holly and other early rockers catered to a new teenage market that had money for the first time, but usually not enough to afford expensive albums. Neat and compact compared to 'old-fashioned' 78s, the record boom triggered by early rock guaranteed the success of the new format as the standard vehicle for singles in every genre.

RELATED TOPICS
See also
THE FIRST ROCK 'N' ROLL RECORD
page 28

CLASSIC ROCK 'N' ROLL
page 36

ELVIS PRESLEY: 'HEARTBREAK HOTEL'
page 116

3-SECOND BIOGRAPHIES
THOMAS EDISON
1847–1931
Inventor of the 'Phonograph', a key pioneer in the development of the domestic record player

BING CROSBY
1903–77
Pre-rock 'crooner', his version of 'White Christmas' (1942) is still the biggest-selling single of all time

30-SECOND TEXT
Mike Evans

Pioneer rockers like Elvis, seen here in Jailhouse Rock, owed their entire success to the sales of singles.

THE ALBUM

the 30-second rock

Although the long-playing album was introduced in the late 1940s, for its first ten years or so rock music was dominated by the single, albums being either 'greatest hits' collections or a luxury only extended to the most successful acts. It was in the latter half of the 1960s, when performers such as Bob Dylan (*Bringing It All Back Home*, 1965), the Beach Boys (*Pet Sounds*, 1966) and the Beatles (*Revolver*, 1966) made the 12-inch 'long-player' a work of art, that the rock album came into its own. By the end of the decade, new 'underground' acts such as Jefferson Airplane (*Surrealistic Pillow*, 1967) and Janis Joplin (*I Got Dem Ol' Kozmic Blues Again Mama!*, 1969) were almost exclusively identified by their albums. Into the 1970s, heavy rock pioneers Led Zeppelin (*Led Zeppelin III*, 1970) insisted on album-only releases, while 'progressive' rock was characterized by ambitious concepts and rock operas that extended to double- or even treble-disc packages. And packaging became an art form in itself, with influential visual artists like Roger Dean (Yes, *Tales from Topographic Oceans*, 1973) and Hipgnosis (Pink Floyd, *Dark Side of the Moon*, 1973) being almost as celebrated as their musical clients. As the recent vinyl revival demonstrates, sleeve design was never the same in the context of the 5-inch CD.

3-SECOND LICK
Since the late 1960s, the album rather than the single has been the dominant format for rock music, from progressive to new wave, and heavy metal to indie.

3-MINUTE JAM
Many key albums had iconic covers to match, such as Elvis's debut LP (*Elvis Presley*, 1956) with its action-packed photo and day-glo typography, and Robert Freeman's black-and-white portraits on *With the Beatles* (1963). Psychedelic rock produced mind-bending imagery (Cream, *Disraeli Gears*, 1967), while artists such as Andy Warhol (Rolling Stones, *Sticky Fingers*, 1971) have created memorable sleeves. And punk's graphic image was immortalized forever in Jamie Read's *Never Mind the Bollocks, Here's the Sex Pistols* in 1977.

RELATED TOPICS
See also
THE BEATLES
page 40

PROGRESSIVE ROCK
page 42

KEY CROSSOVERS
page 88

AOR ROCK
page 104

3-SECOND BIOGRAPHIES
EDWARD WALLERSTEIN
1891–1970
Record executive. As boss of Columbia Records, he developed the first long-playing album, launched on 18 June 1948 in New York City

ROGER DEAN
1944–
Illustrator who worked on album covers for prog rock bands including Yes, Uriah Heep, Gentle Giant and Asia

30-SECOND TEXT
Mike Evans

Extravagant album packaging has included coloured vinyl and Warhol's 'zip fastener' cover for the Stones.

PRODUCERS

the 30-second rock

In the rock 'n' roll era, the first producer of note was Sun Records' Sam Phillips. He encouraged blues talent like Ike Turner, Howlin' Wolf and Rufus Thomas to record at his tiny Memphis studio. But when Elvis Presley sauntered in, in July 1953, the world soon turned. In his wake came Johnny Cash, Jerry Lee Lewis and Carl Perkins, all looking for a bit of that Phillips magic. Phil Spector saw himself creating 'mini symphonies for kids' with his Wagnerian early-1960s pop singles for the Crystals, Ronettes and Righteous Brothers; defiantly sticking to mono rather than stereo, Spector revolutionized record production. EMI staff producer George Martin lucked onto a Liverpudlian quartet in 1962, and for seven years was the only producer the Beatles truly trusted. Martin's productions, drawing on his classical background and willingness to experiment, enriched such sonic soundscapes as *Revolver* and *Sgt. Pepper*. The new technology of the 1970s saw artists take production into their own hands, while latterly, Chris Thomas could switch from Roxy Music to the Sex Pistols. In the 1980s and 1990s, John Leckie shaped the sound of the Stone Roses and Radiohead. Twenty-first-century developments, both in home computers and recording science, have seen the traditional role of the record producer diminish somewhat.

RELATED TOPICS
See also
THE ALBUM
page 60

ELVIS PRESLEY: 'HEARTBREAK HOTEL'
page 116

THE BEATLES: *REVOLVER*
page 120

BLONDIE: *PARALLEL LINES*
page 126

3-SECOND BIOGRAPHIES
JOHN HAMMOND
1910–87
Pioneered the early recordings of important jazz and rock artists, including Billie Holiday, Aretha Franklin and Bob Dylan

SAM PHILLIPS
1923–2003
Pioneering producer, notable for his work with blues acts before working with Elvis Presley, Jerry Lee Lewis, Carl Perkins and Johnny Cash

30-SECOND TEXT
Patrick Humphries

3-SECOND LICK
As rock became more sophisticated, so did the role of the producer. Many of the Beatles' later recordings, for instance, simply couldn't be reproduced on stage.

3-MINUTE JAM
The role of the record producer was first really noticed in the 1960s with Phil Spector's thunderous pop hits. The Beatles' work with George Martin at Abbey Road and, in the 1970s, Pink Floyd and Queen at the same studio, demonstrated how music was harnessing the new technology. In recent years, state-of-the-art hardware has meant that many acts have been able to replicate the sound of the studio at home.

A spectral Phil Spector hovers above the dapper George Martin.

1962
Jagger, Jones and Richards form the 'Rollin' Stones', playing their first gig at London's Marquee Club

1965–7
Height of their early fame – singles and albums regularly top the charts, they tour worldwide

1971
With their ninth studio album, *Sticky Fingers*, they form Rolling Stones Records

2016
Blue and Lonesome, covering blues songs from their youth, is number one worldwide

1963
Recommended by the Beatles' George Harrison, they sign with Decca Records

1967
Jagger and Richards arrested for drug possession and are sentenced to jail, though sentences later reduced

1975
Following Taylor's departure, ex-Faces guitarist Ronnie Wood joins the band

1964
Chart success follows: 'I Wanna Be Your Man', 'Not Fade Away', and their first number one, 'It's All Over Now'

1969
Jones, replaced by Mick Taylor a month earlier, dies on the night of 3 July

1980s–2000s
Position confirmed as the world's top touring rock act

THE ROLLING STONES

On 5 July 1969, following the death of their guitarist Brian Jones, the Rolling Stones were introduced to a quarter of a million fans at a free concert in London's Hyde Park as 'the greatest rock and roll band in the world'. How and why they were great, and how long the greatness really lasted, have been much discussed – but even if they'd split at the end of the 1960s, their place in music history would have been secure. For at their height, they rocked like nobody else.

Brian Jones (1942–69), with his passion for the blues developed in the unlikely outpost of Cheltenham, moved to London where he met, among others on the capital's R&B scene, Mick Jagger (1943–) and Keith Richards (1943–) from Dartford, and subsequently bass player Bill Wyman (1936–). The early history of the Stones revolves around the creative sparks and tensions which flowed from that first meeting, in which Jones's commitment to authentic blues based on Muddy Waters and Jimmy Reed was eventually overshadowed by the development of Jagger and Richards as a songwriting team, encouraged by their young manager, Andrew Loog Oldham.

Oldham also promoted a 'bad boy' image for the group, matched by Jagger's on-stage gyrations and snarling vocals. Always lyrically and musically rougher and rawer than the rest, the Stones seemed equally as satisfied with notoriety as they were with fame; their early years provided plenty of material for the scandal sheets, with tales of drug-fuelled excess regularly hitting the headlines. And a month after leaving the group in June 1969, Brian Jones was found dead in the swimming pool at his home.

Their mid-period with Mick Taylor (1949–) on guitar produced some of their most mature and memorable work. *Exile on Main Street* (1971) is regarded by many as their greatest album, while the singles 'Honky Tonk Women' (1969), 'Brown Sugar' (1971) and 'Tumbling Dice' (1972) charted massively around the world.

Their celebrity assured and their musical achievement recognized, the group became part of the rock establishment that punk was to challenge, though they would still surprise with excursions into funk ('Miss You', 1978) and country ('Faraway Eyes', 1978). The Stones have rocked and rolled, endured and survived, with surprising longevity; Jagger, Richards, Ronnie Wood (1947–) and drummer Charlie Watts (1941–) continue to perform and record well into their seventh decade. The energy levels may not quite be the same as in their 1960s heyday, but their love of the music and determination to keep rocking remain undimmed.

Hugh Weldon

SONGWRITERS
the 30-second rock

The components of a successful record are artist, musicians, song and production but nowadays the quality of the song is often marginalized. The best songs articulate emotion in a way that their listeners never could: most couples have 'our song', and favourite records such as 'My Way' are even played at funerals. Carole King and Gerry Goffin expressed teenage angst in classics like 'Will You Love Me Tomorrow', while Lennon and McCartney raised their own standards in response to competing material from Brian Wilson, Bob Dylan and Burt Bacharach. Most rock groups endeavoured to write their own material, overturning the Tin Pan Alley tradition of a separation between songwriters and performers. Not being writers, Frank Sinatra and Elvis Presley, for instance, depended on material from professional writers, and Presley's career suffered when he neglected to pick good songs. Many songs reflect, and also transcend, the time in which they were written, such as Eddie Cochran's 'Summertime Blues' (1960), Sam Cooke's 'A Change Is Gonna Come' (1964) and 'Going Underground' by The Jam (1980). Many folk-based writers wrote about social injustice, while Bob Dylan and Leonard Cohen established that rock lyrics could be poetry, and the singer-songwriter became a genre in its own right.

RELATED TOPICS
See also
REBEL, REBEL: ROCK AS PROTEST MUSIC
page 84

BOB DYLAN
page 86

3-SECOND BIOGRAPHIES
CHUCK BERRY
1926–2017
Poet laureate and riff-meister of 1950s rock 'n' roll

LEONARD COHEN
1934–2016
Singer-songwriter who wrote classics such as 'Suzanne', 'Bird on the Wire' and 'Hallelujah'

CAROLE KING
1942–
Wrote innumerable pop hits and recorded the multi-million-selling *Tapestry* (1971)

30-SECOND TEXT
Spencer Leigh

Chuck Berry celebrating schooldays, Leonard Cohen merging the sacred with the sexual, and Bob Dylan, who called his protest songs, 'finger-pointin' songs'.

3-SECOND LICK
Rock songs can tell stories, express romantic sentiments and reflect social concerns. The best ones are melodic poetry that can make the whole world sing.

3-MINUTE JAM
Artists as diverse as Chuck Berry, Lennon and McCartney, Bob Dylan, David Bowie, Joni Mitchell and Kanye West have something important in common – they all know how to express emotions and thoughts in one three-minute song. And while rock is often seen as a male-dominated world, the emergence of female singer-songwriters like Carole King, Joni Mitchell and Suzanne Vega has encouraged a more balanced state of affairs.

ROCK ON THE ROAD

the 30-second rock

3-SECOND LICK
Recordings are the essential medium of rock music, but for an act to really be considered 'performers' they have to be experienced live.

3-MINUTE JAM
The 'Chitlin' Circuit' was a crucial string of clubs and theatres that catered for African-Americans in the segregated USA, named after the 'chitterlings' (made from pig intestines) typically served at the venues. Until the civil rights movement of the 1960s, many regular establishments didn't admit black audiences, giving rise to the Circuit, on which artists like Jimi Hendrix, James Brown and Ike and Tina Turner all cut their teeth.

Most musicians start out playing small local venues, which are usually the best places to communicate with an audience; there are those who swear the Beatles were never better than they were at Liverpool's Cavern Club, and it's no surprise that when a major act chooses to play a 'secret' show, they usually do so at a small club. But if a band limits their gigging to the local bar, the act will remain a hobby, not a profession; you've got to get out on the road. Hence the circuit of small venues open to touring acts. Larger theatres and ballrooms offer more amenities (like seating and working bathrooms), but still retain some intimacy. At arena shows, it's more about the event, the communal spirit of an audience united for a single purpose. Live shows create a bond between the performer and audience that's unique. It's why people follow a favourite act on tour (think of the Grateful Dead's 'Deadheads'), or travelled halfway around the world to see Kate Bush's much-anticipated live shows in 2014. And it's why 'heritage' acts like the Rolling Stones, that no longer have to play live to earn money, still can't resist the lure of the road.

RELATED TOPICS
See also
BEAT, BLUES & FOLK ROCK
page 38

PROGRESSIVE ROCK
page 42

LANDMARK GIGS
page 70

3-SECOND BIOGRAPHIES
DICK CLARK
1929–2012
Radio and TV personality whose 'Caravan of Stars', launched in 1959, boasted racially integrated package shows of top stars

BILL GRAHAM
1931–91
Rock promoter whose venues (Fillmore West, Fillmore East, Winterland Arena) were – and still are – key stops for touring musicians

30-SECOND TEXT
Gillian G. Gaar

Hitting the road is a key way a band can take itself from being a hobby to a profession.

LANDMARK GIGS

the 30-second rock

A 'landmark show' is a key event; something confirming the popularity of a new act, or presenting music in a new way, to a new audience. Elvis Presley's 13 May 1955 show in Jacksonville, Florida, provoked a riot, establishing Presley as a rising star. The Beatles' concert at Shea Stadium in New York on 15 August 1965, drew their biggest audience, and marked the moment when stadium rock became viable. The Monterey Pop Festival, held 16–18 June 1967, boosted the careers of Janis Joplin, The Who and Jimi Hendrix. Events like the Woodstock Music & Art Fair (15–18 August 1969 in Bethel, New York) and the Wattstax concert (20 August 1972, in Los Angeles) sought to build and celebrate a sense of community, while George Harrison's charity concerts for Bangladesh (two shows held 1 August 1971 in New York City), were the first large-scale benefit rock promotions, laying the groundwork for future events such as the Bob Geldof-organized Live Aid shows, held on 13 July 1985, in London and Philadelphia. But most landmark gigs are about the performance, not the cause: Nirvana's remarkable appearance on *MTV Unplugged* on 18 November 1993, or Oasis's two shows at the UK's Knebworth Festival (10 and 11 August 1996), which made them a major act.

3-SECOND LICK
A number of rock shows haven't just provided entertainment – they've also made it into the history books for a variety of reasons.

3-MINUTE JAM
Some shows become 'landmarks' for what went wrong; Bob Dylan being booed for 'going electric' at the Newport Folk Festival on 25 July 1965, or The Doors' lead singer Jim Morrison charged with indecent exposure at a Miami concert on 1 March 1969. Other mishaps have been more serious. During the Rolling Stones' set at the Altamont Speedway Free Festival in Tracy, California, on 6 December 1969, a fan was stabbed to death, as documented in the film *Gimme Shelter*.

RELATED TOPIC
See also
ROCK ON THE ROAD
page 68

3-SECOND BIOGRAPHIES
JIM MORRISON
1943–71
Charismatic lead singer and songwriter with The Doors

BOB GELDOF
1951–
Activist and campaigner who co-organized the Band Aid charity record (1984), and Live Aid concerts in 1985

30-SECOND TEXT
Gillian G. Gaar

A landmark gig isn't just a show; it makes history. The Beatles at Shea Stadium in 1965, (top) and the 1969 Woodstock Festival (bottom).

ROCK CULTURE

ROCK CULTURE
GLOSSARY

auto-tune An audio processing technology that alters the pitch in vocal and instrumental recordings. Originally intended to correct out-of-tune performances, it has been used to 'perfect' recordings to the extent that they can sometimes lose their true character.

compression A process in digital recording that reduces the dynamic range in an audio signal by boosting the quietest elements and lessening the loudest, thereby making it possible to increase the actual overall volume within the limits of a particular piece of equipment. The downside is a noticeable loss of 'edge' in some cases, making for a blander feel to the final output.

double album A vinyl album consisting of two discs, to accommodate up to twice the normal playing time, usually packaged in a double 'gatefold' sleeve.

Goth Teen subculture which began in the UK as an offshoot of the post-punk rock scene, with prominent associated musical names including Siouxsie and the Banshees, Bauhaus and the Cure. Goth fashion is characterized by dark elements such as predominantly all-black clothing, dyed black hair, dark eyeliner and black nail varnish.

groovebox A self-contained device that includes a sound source such as a drum machine or synthesizer, a music sequencer and a control board. With these features integrated into one system, the musician can build up a sequence of instrumental or percussion elements playing in tandem.

hepcat Originating in 1930s African-American jazz subculture, similar in meaning to 'hipster' (not to be confused with modern-day hipsters) in the 1940s and 1950s jazz and 'beatnik' scene. Usually referred to someone considered a 'cool' character, and/or a fashionable dresser.

looping The use of short sections of music (or other sound) repeated continuously, to get a desired – often 'hypnotic' – effect. The term originates from tape looping, but now a loop can be created by many music technologies including digital samplers, drum machines, synthesizers and so on.

Mellotron An electronic keyboard launched in England in the 1960s that used tape-recorded replay to achieve a variety of effects.

mod Mod originated as a subculture in late 1950s London, its predominantly male members being fans of modern jazz (hence the name), dressing in neat Italian-inspired suits, and often riding Italian motor scooters. In the early 1960s mods embraced the emerging R&B scene and the bands associated with it, and by the middle of the decade a whole fashion-conscious teenage sub-group, identified with rock bands like The Who and the Small Faces, was now labelled 'mod'.

quantization Digital recording process that 'corrects' imprecisely performed notes in terms of their exact timing.

rockumentary Film or television documentary where the subject is rock music and rock musicians.

sitar A plucked stringed instrument featured in Indian classical music. Its most celebrated exponent was Ravi Shankar, whose tuition of George Harrison led to its adoption in 1960s rock music, including major records by the Beatles, the Rolling Stones and The Doors.

Summer of Love A prelude to the Summer of Love was in January 1967 with a gathering of the 'flower children' in San Francisco's Golden Gate Park called the Human Be-In, followed in the UK by the 14-Hour Technicolour Dream event in London on 29 April. The phrase was used specifically to describe the influx of thousands of hippies who descended on the Haight-Ashbury district of San Francisco during the summer of 1967. More generally, it referred to the summer months of that year, beginning with the release of the Beatles' *Sgt. Pepper's Lonely Hearts Club Band* in the June, and events like the Monterey Pop Festival (which included the Grateful Dead, Jefferson Airplane, Jimi Hendrix and Janis Joplin), that were a catalyst for the emerging counterculture of the late 1960s.

FOLLOWERS OF FASHION

the 30-second rock

3-SECOND LICK
Rock fashion is about rebellion from the humdrum and from whatever came before. In rock, clothes don't make the man, or woman. But they help.

3-MINUTE JAM
Over the years, London has left an indelible mark on rock fashion. Carnaby Street clothiers defined the mod style of the mid-1960s, while later in the decade Granny Takes a Trip (King's Road) and Mr. Fish (Mayfair) outfitted the Rolling Stones, David Bowie and many more. At the Sex boutique on King's Road, in the late 1970s Vivienne Westwood pioneered punk fashion in her then-outrageous styles for the Sex Pistols and others.

Fashion has been a key element of rock ever since Elvis Presley shook his mighty hips. He dressed flamboyantly like the black hepcats he admired, wearing striped or leather jackets, and pink or black shirts with the collar roguishly turned up. The Beatles popularized long hair for men and numerous fashion looks, as their sartorial style evolved with their sound, from staid matching suits to Carnaby Street mod finery. Hippie style came to full flower in 1967's Summer of Love, and clothing followed suit with multicoloured trousers, flowing shirts and bright scarves as likely to be seen on men as women. The Rolling Stones and Robert Plant of Led Zeppelin wore women's blouses and scarves to achieve an androgynous balance of masculine and feminine. Glam rockers like David Bowie deliberately tipped that balance to effeminate with dyed hair, mascara, lipstick, satin fabrics, feather boas and platform shoes. Punk rock garb was as tough and aggressive as its sound. Safety-pins, mohawks, torn T-shirts, spiked collars and leather all signified punk's defiance. In the 1980s, the 'paint it black' attitude of Goth style evolved from punk and heavy metal. Emo fashion sprouted from a different branch of punk, and offered skinny jeans, tight T-shirts, and other nerdy clothes sported by emo bands such as Weezer. What's next? Turn, turn, turn …

RELATED TOPICS
See also
ELVIS PRESLEY
page 26

THE BEATLES
page 40

PUNK & NEW WAVE
page 46

GLAM ROCK
page 102

DAVID BOWIE
page 146

3-SECOND BIOGRAPHIES
MICHAEL FISH
1940–
Owner of boutique Mr. Fish and fashion designer for the Rolling Stones and David Bowie

VIVIENNE WESTWOOD
1941–
Partner of Malcolm McLaren in the Sex boutique, punk rock fashion pioneer and haute couture fashion designer

30-SECOND TEXT
Paul Kingsbury

Rock stars have always distinguished themselves from their fans through their finery.

ROCK AT THE MOVIES

the 30-second rock

3-SECOND LICK
Since the 1950s, rock music of one kind or another has provided the soundtrack to all our lives, as well as the soundtrack to some key movies.

3-MINUTE JAM
Bill Haley's 'Rock Around the Clock' anticipated the rock revolution in mid-1955, when it was used over the credits for the high-school delinquency drama *Blackboard Jungle*. Since then rock has often been used effectively in otherwise non-musical films, such as the Crystals' 'And Then He Kissed Me' in Scorsese's *Goodfellas* (1990), Chuck Berry's 'You Never Can Tell' in Quentin Tarantino's *Pulp Fiction* (1994) and Blur, Primal Scream and other alt-rock names in Danny Boyle's *Trainspotting* (1996).

The earliest movies featuring rock 'n' roll were cheap exploitation films like *Rock Around the Clock* (1956) and *Don't Knock the Rock* (1957) – both of which featured Bill Haley, DJ Alan Freed and a string of hitmakers in cameo performances, linked together with a flimsy plot. Of those early rock films, only the satirical *The Girl Can't Help It* (1956) has stood the test of time. But it was the Beatles' day-in-the-life comedy *A Hard Day's Night* (1964), by the acclaimed director Richard Lester, that saw the rock film raised to a new level. Rock biopics have proliferated over the years, with Oliver Stone's *The Doors* (1991) and *Control* (2007) – about Joy Division's Ian Curtis – being among the best. Similarly, renowned directors have tackled 'rockumentaries', including Martin Scorsese with The Band's farewell concert in *The Last Waltz* (1978), and D.A. Pennebaker's record of Bob Dylan's 1965 UK tour in *Don't Look Back* (1967). And there are movies that address the essence of rock 'n' roll, including *Quadrophenia* (1979) based on The Who album, actor John Cusack's portrayal of a record-collector obsessive in *High Fidelity* (2000), Alan Parker's account of an Irish soul band in *The Commitments* (1991) and, of course, the ultimate heavy metal send-up in Rob Reiner's 1984 'mockumentary' *This Is Spinal Tap*.

RELATED TOPICS
See also
THE BIRTH OF THE TEENAGER
page 30

HEAVY METAL
page 44

3-SECOND BIOGRAPHIES
SAM KATZMAN
1901–73
Veteran producer specializing in low-budget movies, including the seminal *Rock Around the Clock* (1956)

RICHARD LESTER
1932–
Film director, music-related films include *A Hard Day's Night* (1964) and *Help!* (1965)

MARTIN SCORSESE
1942–
Film director, documentaries include Dylan (*No Direction Home*, 2005) and the Stones (*Shine a Light*, 2008)

30-SECOND TEXT
Mike Evans

Rock-influenced directors have included Martin Scorsese (top), Alan Parker (right) and Richard Lester (left).

ROCK LITERATURE

the 30-second rock

Any writing about rock 'n' roll, as it was unfolding in the 1950s, was inadequate. It appeared only in newspapers, fan magazines and trade papers; nobody, not even most of the performers, thought it was going to last. A breakthrough came with Michael Braun's book about touring with the Beatles, *Love Me Do*, in 1964, followed in 1968 by the only authorized biography of the band, by Hunter Davies. Inspired by the nonsense verse of Spike Milligan, John Lennon wrote the best-selling *In His Own Write* (1964) and *A Spaniard in the Works* (1965), and Bob Dylan offered the unfathomable *Tarantula* (1971). On another level was Charlie Gillett's *The Sound of the City* (1971), the untold study of the US record industry, while Nik Cohn offered a highly opinionated pop history, *Awopbopaloobop Alopbamboom* (1972). Since then, there have been many scholarly biographies from expert writers including Peter Guralnick (Elvis), Mark Lewisohn (Beatles), Michael Gray (Bob Dylan) and David Buckley (David Bowie). It is now commonplace for rock musicians to write autobiographies, and there have been bestsellers from Pete Townshend, Brian Wilson, Keith Richards, Bob Dylan and Bruce Springsteen. The next trend could be fictional stories around factual musicians, such as Steve Bergsman's engaging *The Death of Johnny Ace* (2014).

RELATED TOPICS
See also
LANDMARK GIGS
page 70

ROCK AT THE MOVIES
page 78

BRUCE SPRINGSTEEN
page 106

3-SECOND BIOGRAPHIES
PETER GURALNICK
1943–
Acclaimed biographer of Elvis Presley and Sam Phillips

GREIL MARCUS
1945–
Opinionated, academic and with a style that is the holy Greil for aspiring rock writers; *Mystery Train* (1975) is still his masterwork

MARK LEWISOHN
1958–
Forensic researcher and biographer of the Beatles

30-SECOND TEXT
Spencer Leigh

A new genre of rock literature has developed, from biographies to academic studies and quiz books.

3-SECOND LICK
Since the 1960s, a growth industry has developed around music books, with fans wanting to know about rock's history, and the lives of the musicians themselves.

3-MINUTE JAM
Rock biographies, especially the more salacious ones, now vie with show business biographies for the top of the bestseller lists. There is also a serious demand from customers who want to know how their favourite records were made, and how the different genres of rock came into being and have developed – but after several hundred books, is there anything more to be said about the Beatles?

WOMEN IN ROCK

the 30-second rock

The road to superstardom

enjoyed by the likes of Adele and Taylor Swift was paved with the sweat and tears of their forerunners. In the 1950s, rockabilly belters like Brenda Lee and Wanda Jackson revealed a scorching style all their own, but few female rockers made it big back then. By the 1960s, women found easier inroads in 'girl groups', though typically produced and managed by men. Thus, Berry Gordy at Motown guided the Supremes and Martha & the Vandellas, while Phil Spector produced the Crystals and Ronettes. Initially, Carole King and Joni Mitchell wrote songs for others, before becoming hit artists in their own right. A sea change came in the late 1960s, when strong women like Grace Slick and Janis Joplin fronted rock bands as lead singers. Their success opened doors in the 1970s and 1980s for Stevie Nicks and Christine McVie of Fleetwood Mac, sisters Ann and Nancy Wilson of Heart, and Debbie Harry of Blondie, as well as solo artists like Linda Ronstadt. Since then adventurous rock performers including Patti Smith, Lucinda Williams and Madonna have influenced women and men alike. Today, when a PJ Harvey or St. Vincent dazzles with guitar, vocals, production or songwriting, no one is surprised – which may be the biggest breakthrough of all.

30-SECOND TEXT
Paul Kingsbury

Women have been key creators from rock's beginning, but they have only recently been able to call the shots.

REBEL REBEL: ROCK AS PROTEST MUSIC

the 30-second rock

Ever since Bob Dylan 'went
electric' in 1965 and took his folk-protest music
into the rock 'n' roll arena, rock has been used as
a potent vehicle of political and social dissent.
Dylan had already written some of the greatest
political songs of the era, such as 'Masters of
War' and 'Blowin' in the Wind', both having
appeared on his second album, *The Freewheelin'*
Bob Dylan (1963). But as the decade progressed,
so did the war in Vietnam, and the emerging
counterculture produced bands like Country Joe
and the Fish, whose 'I-Feel-Like-I'm-Fixin'-to-
Die Rag' (1967) was an anthem against the
military conscription of America's male youth.
In the 'progressive' music of the early 1970s,
protest was largely muted, until punk noisily
burst onto the scene in 1976, most notably in
the UK with The Clash, whose politically charged
albums included *The Clash* (1977) and *London
Calling* (1979). And in Germany, the 'Deutschpunk'
movement was represented famously by Slime,
the first band to have its album banned because
of its radical lyrics. More recently, alternative
and indie rock has provided a regular platform
for protest, including the Canadian band Arcade
Fire (*Neon Bible*, 2007) and Welsh seditionaries
the Manic Street Preachers – whose strident
outrage spans three decades, from *Generation
Terrorists* (1992) to *Futurology* (2014).

3-SECOND BIOGRAPHIES
COUNTRY JOE MCDONALD
1942–
Singer-songwriter with Country
Joe and the Fish

JOE STRUMMER
1952–2002
Lead vocalist and songwriter
with The Clash

JAMES DEAN BRADFIELD
1969–
Lead guitarist and vocalist
with Manic Street Preachers

30-SECOND TEXT
Mike Evans

*Radical rock has ranged
from Joan Baez (centre)
supporting Martin
Luther King, to the
punk outrage of The
Clash (top).*

24 May 1941
Born Robert Zimmerman in Minnesota

1961
Arrives in New York, performing as 'Bob Dylan'

1963
Largely self-penned, *Freewheelin'* announces the arrival of a major talent

1964
The Times They Are A-Changin' enshrines Dylan as the era's leading 'protest' singer

1965
Shocks folk fans with his electric albums *Bringing It All Back Home* and *Highway 61 Revisited*

1966
Records in country music capital Nashville. *Blonde on Blonde* is rock's first double album

1966
Out of action for 18 months after motorcycle accident

1969
'Return' gig at UK Isle of Wight Festival

1975
Blood on the Tracks hailed as classic

1979
Conversion as 'born again' Christian

1989
Oh Mercy acclaimed as return to form

2007
Biopic *I'm Not There* released

2012
35th studio album *Tempest* released

2016
Receives Nobel Prize for Literature

BOB DYLAN

No single artist has ever had such impact on rock music as Bob Dylan. It was Dylan who gave pop music a voice, liberating it from the anodyne love song, and instilling a social conscience into the form with early songs such as 'Blowin' in the Wind', 'A Hard Rain's A-Gonna Fall' and 'The Times They Are A-Changin''. Even his love songs ('Don't Think Twice It's Alright', 'It Ain't Me Babe') were coruscatingly fresh, injecting a raw honesty into the format. It was Dylan who virtually invented the concept of singer-songwriter, influencing everyone from Leonard Cohen to Ed Sheeran.

In the mid-1960s, his sudden switch from solo folk singer to electric rocker alienated fans yearning for his 'protest' material, but won him a wider pop audience. The electric six-minute single 'Like a Rolling Stone' (1965) put him into the top ten, shattering all precepts of what a 'pop song' could achieve, while that same year's acoustic 'Mr. Tambourine Man' confirmed him as a poet.

Dylan sent out further shock waves when he became the first rock star to record in the country music capital of Nashville, invoking Hank Williams with albums like *John Wesley Harding* (1968) and *Nashville Skyline* (1969). Never one to be bound by convention or style, Dylan's influence extends across folk, pop, gospel and blues. Many took *Blood on the Tracks* (1975) as his most honest recorded statement.

Over the years, Dylan has moved into film acting and direction, prose writing, painting and sculpture. A patchy period ended with his return to critical and public popularity with disparate albums such as *Oh Mercy* (1989) and *Time Out of Mind* (1997). Without Bob Dylan, most pop lyrics would still be in the nursery. Dylan's willingness to change, experiment and not be bound by expectation has enriched the musical landscape, as he switched from solo folk to electric rock to country music to gospel. His songs have been recorded by everyone from Adele to Neil Young, ensuring a healthy income, yet Dylan never strays far from the concert stage. After Elvis Presley and the Beatles, he is the most written-about rock icon. The 2016 Nobel Prize for Literature confirmed his status as a major cultural force.

Patrick Humphries

KEY CROSSOVERS

the 30-second rock

3-SECOND LICK
Various other musical
styles have mixed and
mashed-up with rock to
create exciting new music
genres in their own right.

3-MINUTE JAM
Miles Davis's so-called
'electric period', from 1968
to 1975, saw the trumpet
giant introducing rock
instrumentation in his
music, and facing some of
the same outrage from jazz
purists that Bob Dylan
faced when he picked up
an electric guitar. But *In a
Silent Way* (1969) and,
especially, *Bitches Brew*
(1970), were credited with
reintroducing jazz, which
had been sidelined during
the rock era, to a new
mainstream audience.

Rock itself was a 'crossover' of rhythm and blues and country music, and once established it began merging with other styles. The mid-1960s saw folk rock emerge, with the 1965 release of the Byrds' cover of Bob Dylan's 'Mr. Tambourine Man' and Simon & Garfunkel's 'The Sound of Silence'. Gram Parsons, who joined the Byrds in 1968, moved the group into country rock on *Sweetheart of the Rodeo*, a genre he further explored in his subsequent group the Flying Burrito Brothers. Other country rock acts included Emmylou Harris, Linda Ronstadt and Michael Nesmith (formerly with The Monkees). Western interest in Indian culture, and the music of sitar player Ravi Shankar, led to the development of raga rock, with the Beatles, the Rolling Stones and the Paul Butterfield Blues Band incorporating Eastern influences in their songs; in the 1990s, UK group Kula Shaker recorded raga rock numbers like 'Govinda'. The Doors and Chicago had elements of jazz in their music, paving the way for the jazz-rock fusion experimentations of Miles Davis, Weather Report and Chick Corea in the 1970s. Rock acts also drew on classical music, with Mason Williams' 'Classical Gas' (1968) and Walter Murphy's 'A Fifth of Beethoven' (1976) being big hits.

RELATED TOPIC
See also
BOB DYLAN: *BRINGING IT ALL
BACK HOME*
page 118

3-SECOND BIOGRAPHIES
RAVI SHANKAR
1920–2012
Indian musician and composer
who influenced numerous
Western musicians

MILES DAVIS
1926–91
Jazz musician and composer
who stretched the musical
boundaries of the genre

GRAM PARSONS
1946–73
Guitarist, singer, songwriter,
member of the Byrds and the
Flying Burrito Brothers

30-SECOND TEXT
Gillian G. Gaar

*Miles Davis (top), Simon
& Garfunkel (middle)
and the Byrds (bottom)
expanded rock's
parameters by
introducing elements
from other genres.*

DIGITAL ROCK – THE FUTURE?

the 30-second rock

'You can't beat guitars, bass and drums,' said Lou Reed in the sleeve note to his 1989 album *New York*. For the rock purist that may still be true, but the technical advances that have expanded the possibilities of music making and made them available to anyone with a phone in their pocket are what drive the contemporary scene. Rock musicians have had a longstanding relationship with technology – the Moody Blues and the Beatles were using the Mellotron in the late 1960s to expand their soundscapes, while advances in recording techniques enabled artists to focus their creativity on the possibilities offered by the studio, rather than on live performance. Innovations such as compression, auto-tune and quantization eased and sped up the recording process, but for many this resulted in a bland product at odds with the rawer roots of rock. The real digital creativity, though, has arguably been home-produced experimentation; while synth pop and rock have continued, with bands like Justice in France and Ladytron in the UK following a traditional career path, rock's future may well be both more participatory and more fragmented. Artificial intelligence, leap motion programs that enable music to be produced by hand gestures, even programming robots to produce their own compositions: fads, or the future?

3-SECOND LICK
Modern technologies have influenced the progress of rock and pop for decades now, but will the sounds of tomorrow depend as much on technical as musical talent?

3-MINUTE JAM
Electronic rock, synth pop, techno and the dance/ambient scene grew in tandem with the tools that enabled them. Simple sequencing of notes played through a groovebox with the rhythm provided by a drum machine helped Aphex Twin build a whole career; looping, which can be done live, enables artists such as Tune Yards' Merrill Garbus to record and repeat drum, ukulele and voice parts as she performs.

RELATED TOPICS
See also
ELECTRO-ROCK
page 48

PRODUCERS
page 62

3-SECOND BIOGRAPHIES
LAURIE ANDERSON
1947–
Composer, performer, electronic music pioneer and inventor of experimental instruments

RICHARD DAVID JAMES
1971–
Electronic and ambient musician and composer

IMOGEN HEAP
1977–
Singer-songwriter, musician and engineer, known for her 'musical gloves'

30-SECOND TEXT
Hugh Weldon

In the digital age, musicians are as likely to be seen with computers and electronic gadgets as with traditional instruments.

ROCK AS POP

ROCK AS POP
GLOSSARY

AM/FM radio AM (amplitude modulation) was the first method developed for making radio transmissions, and is still used worldwide. More susceptible to interference than the more recent FM (frequency modulation) technology, and with a more limited audio fidelity, AM broadcasters now tend to specialize in talk radio and news programming, with FM and digital stations handling music.

androgyny Of indeterminate gender, or the state of being partly male and partly female in appearance.

Brill Building An office building at 1619 Broadway in Manhattan, New York, which was a centre of the American music publishing industry from the late 1930s. Its heyday in the rock 'n' roll era was in the early 1960s, when its name became a shorthand term for the mainstream pop style of such writers and composers as Neil Sedaka, Bert Berns, Gerry Goffin and Carole King, Burt Bacharach and Hal David, Cynthia Weil and Barry Mann, and Jerry Leiber and Mike Stoller.

British Invasion Journalistic term for the huge assault of UK artists on the US charts in the wake of the Beatles, and subsequent 'invasion' of live touring bands. Major names included the Rolling Stones, the Dave Clark Five and Herman's Hermits, as well as solo names such as Tom Jones, Petula Clark and Donovan. In June 1965, no fewer than 14 British records occupied the US top forty. A big influence on US guitar-led groups of the mid-1960s, including the Beach Boys, Lovin' Spoonful and the Byrds.

doo-wop A vocal group style that emerged in the early days of classic rock 'n' roll, featuring (mainly male) harmony line-ups of four or five singers, typically with a tenor voice singing lead and a bass singer repeating backing lyrics or simple non-verbal phrases (from which came the onomatopoeic name).

falsetto A vocal delivery that is unusually high. In male tenor vocalists, a technique of reaching notes usually above their normal range.

grunge Specifically describing the alternative rock of 1990s (mainly) Seattle bands including Nirvana, Soundgarden and Pearl Jam, and similar groups who followed in their wake.

hook A catchy chorus, repeated instrumental figure or bridge passage between verses, which almost literally 'hooks' the listener into a pop song.

jam band A style of rock group that first appeared in the late 1960s, whose live appearances featured lengthy 'jams' on stage, with extravagant guitar and drum solos. Typified by concerts (and live albums) by the Grateful Dead, Allman Brothers Band and others.

mod Mod originated as a subculture in late 1950s London, its predominantly male members being fans of modern jazz (hence the name), dressing in neat Italian-inspired suits, and often riding Italian motor scooters. In the early 1960s mods embraced the emerging R&B scene and the bands associated with it, and by the middle of the decade a whole fashion-conscious teenage sub-group, identified with rock bands like The Who and the Small Faces, was now labelled 'mod'.

Radio Luxembourg Radio station located in the small European country of Luxembourg. In the 1950s it played a key role in broadcasting rock music to UK audiences, while the domestic BBC service almost ignored the new music entirely.

session singer With a working relationship similar to a session musician, a freelance professional vocalist who is hired (often on a session-by-session basis) to contribute to studio recordings, usually in a backing capacity.

staccato A style of musical delivery where each note or short phrase is sharply detached from those preceding or following it, giving an emphasis to the individual elements while achieving a machine-like repetition if delivered at speed.

SURF MUSIC

the 30-second rock

3-SECOND LICK
Via surf music, the world's
youth was presented with
the idyllic notion of life
on a California beach as
a paradise on Earth.

3-MINUTE JAM
Surf music, alongside
hot rod music, was an
early-1960s Californian
phenomenon split into
two strands: the joyous,
warm harmonies of the
Beach Boys and Jan and
Dean, and the tense,
surfing instrumentals from
Dick Dale, the Chantays
and the Surfaris. There
was no hint of protest or
rebellion in the songs, and
right then American youth
had never had it so good –
but Vietnam was just
around the corner.

In 1961, as the California group
the Beach Boys were recording their first single,
their drummer Dennis Wilson remarked, 'No
one's ever written a song about surfing' and
lights went up all around. Brian Wilson and Mike
Love wrote 'Surfin'', and soon they were on a
roll with idyllic songs about California girls, the
warmth of the sun and having fun, fun, fun.
Their friends Jan and Dean topped the US charts
in 1963 with Brian Wilson's 'Surf City', the
chorus embodying every young man's dream:
'two girls for every boy'. The Trashmen scored
with the nonsensical 'Surfin' Bird' and there
was instrumental music from the Chantays
('Pipeline') and the Surfaris ('Wipe Out'). Dick
Dale, billed as the King of the Surf Guitar and
based at the Rendezvous Ballroom in Balboa,
developed a staccato-style akin to riding waves,
notably heard in 'Miserlou' (1962). Starting with
Gidget (1959), there was also a spate of beach
party films, often starring Frankie Avalon and
Annette Funicello. It wasn't always an endless
summer for the Beach Boys, and their internal
problems led to 'Surf's Up' in 1971. Jimi Hendrix
wrote 'You'll never hear surf music again' in
'Third Stone from the Sun' (1967), but he was
either wrong or being ironic as every summer
the Beach Boys' hits still fill the airwaves.

RELATED TOPICS
See also
THE BIRTH OF THE TEENAGER
page 30

BEAT, BLUES & FOLK ROCK
page 38

SONGWRITERS
page 66

FOLLOWERS OF FASHION
page 76

3-SECOND BIOGRAPHIES
DICK DALE
1937–
The self-acclaimed King
of the Surf Guitar

BRIAN WILSON
1942–
Wrote, performed and
produced many surf records
with the Beach Boys

DENNIS WILSON
1943–83
Drummer, and the only Beach
Boy who actually surfed

30-SECOND TEXT
Spencer Leigh

*The Beach Boys rode
the waves of surf music.*

GIRL GROUPS

the 30-second rock

3-SECOND LICK
Over the years, girl groups have been the mouthpiece of rock anthems from a female standpoint, in a business dominated by male artists, writers and producers.

3-MINUTE JAM
Masterminded by producer George 'Shadow' Morton, in the mid-1960s the Shangri-Las were the undisputed purveyors of teen trauma. In productions enhanced with sound effects, a string of tear-jerking hits addressed such emotive issues as lost love ('Remember (Walking in the Sand)'), delinquency ('Leader of the Pack'), a teenage runaway ('I Can Never Go Home Anymore'), elopement ('Give Us Your Blessings') and the spine-chilling evocation of sexual angst 'Past, Present and Future'.

The original template for the female vocal group was created in the 1930s by the Boswell Sisters, and their wartime successors the Andrews Sisters – whose many hits included the 1941 best-seller 'Boogie Woogie Bugle Boy'. But the classic girl group sound evolved from the male-dominated doo-wop groups of the early rock 'n' roll era, first hitting the charts in 1958 with 'Maybe' by the Chantels. The format really began to take off in the early 1960s, when Gerry Goffin, Carole King and other songwriters in New York's Brill Building crafted hits for various female line-ups, including 'Will You Love Me Tomorrow' by the Shirelles, and the Chiffons' 'He's So Fine'. And with his 'three-minute symphonies', producer Phil Spector revolutionized pop with studio-created groups including the Ronettes ('Be My Baby', 1963) and the Crystals ('Da Doo Ron Ron', 1963). In Detroit the Motown sound was forged with the Marvelettes, Supremes and many more, while the Red Bird label launched the queens of adolescent angst, the Shangri-Las. Through the 1970s and 1980s, girl groups ranged from soul acts like the Pointer Sisters to the R&B dance music of Exposé. Via the Spice Girls in the 1990s, girl groups have continued to flourish, with the likes of the Sugababes and Fifth Harmony continuing a tradition as old as pop itself.

RELATED TOPICS
See also
GOSPEL & DOO-WOP
page 22

WOMEN IN ROCK
page 82

MOTOWN
page 100

3-SECOND BIOGRAPHIES
PHIL SPECTOR
1939–
Created symphonic sound with early-1960s girl groups the Ronettes and the Crystals

RICHARD 'BIFF' STANNARD
1966–
Songwriter-producer behind the Spice Girls' success, whose 1996 debut album *Spice* was the biggest-selling girl group album ever

30-SECOND TEXT
Mike Evans

Girl Power, from top to bottom: the Boswell Sisters (1930s), the Ronettes and the Supremes (1960s), and the Spice Girls (1990s).

MOTOWN

the 30-second rock

In 1959 Berry Gordy launched his Tamla label in Detroit, and its first major US hits were the Miracles' 'Shop Around' in 1960, and the Marvelettes' 'Please Mr. Postman' in 1961. Gordy started a companion label, Motown (short for Motortown), and had early successes with the Contours' 'Do You Love Me' (1962) and Mary Wells's 'My Guy' in 1964. With songwriting/production team, Holland-Dozier-Holland, one hit followed another for the Supremes, Marvin Gaye, the Four Tops and Martha & the Vandellas. Levi Stubbs bellowed through the Four Tops' 'Reach Out I'll Be There' (1966), written and produced by Norman Whitfield. Whitfield also wrote 'War' for the Temptations, questioning US involvement in Vietnam, re-recording it as a 1970 number one for Edwin Starr on the Gordy label. Gordy counselled Marvin Gaye against releasing the politically charged *What's Going On* (1971), which became a major seller. Stevie Wonder likewise followed his own path, culminating in *Songs in the Key of Life* in 1976. In 1972 Tamla-Motown moved to Los Angeles, where Gordy produced the movie *Lady Sings the Blues*, starring Diana Ross as Billie Holiday. Ross discovered the Jackson 5, but the label began to lose its identity. When people say 'Motown', they are recalling the 1960s version – the basis of the hit show, *Motown: The Musical*.

3-SECOND LICK
Associated with Detroit, Motown presented black artists to a white market and its success was due to star quality, songwriting, dynamic production and neat choreography.

3-MINUTE JAM
In 1960 Berry Gordy founded the Motown Record Corporation in Detroit, and found that he was so astonishingly good at picking talent – the Supremes, the Four Tops, Stevie Wonder and Marvin Gaye – that he could dub his product as 'The Sound of Young America' as opposed to 'The Sound of Black, Young America'. Once established, Motown took a radical stance on both civil rights issues and the war in Vietnam.

RELATED TOPICS
See also
GOSPEL & DOO-WOP
page 22

PRODUCERS
page 62

GIRL GROUPS
page 98

DETROIT
page 138

3-SECOND BIOGRAPHIES
BERRY GORDY
1929–
Founder of the Tamla-Motown record label

MARVIN GAYE
1939–84
Production-line singer who turned to social commentary

DIANA ROSS
1944–
Lead singer of the Supremes and solo star

30-SECOND TEXT
Spencer Leigh

Three of Motown's biggest-selling acts: Stevie Wonder, Diana Ross and the Four Tops.

GLAM ROCK

the 30-second rock

In the early 1970s, glam (short for glamour) emerged as an antidote to the macho posturing and self-importance of mainstream rock. Whereas most 1970s rockers dressed like their fans in T-shirts and jeans, glam musicians flirted with androgyny and dressed flamboyantly, with mascara and platform shoes standard attire. While jam bands and prog rockers recorded extended meandering tracks, glam rockers generally delivered punchier numbers. Marc Bolan of T. Rex sparked the glam trend in Britain in 1971, with a touch of glitter and swaggering hits like 'Get It On'. David Bowie embraced glam and became its leading light with songs about gay life like 'Queen Bitch', and a stage persona that seemed both feminine and alien. Roxy Music, led by singer Bryan Ferry, expanded glam's standard guitar-oriented palette towards the avant-garde with the synthesizer of Brian Eno and Ferry's piano-derived songwriting. In the USA, Lou Reed, Alice Cooper, Kiss, Iggy Pop and the New York Dolls dressed tough but pretty, and rocked gritty. Other hit-making acts who wore it well in the 1970s include Mott the Hoople, Slade, Sweet and Queen – the latter group artfully blending the power of heavy metal with Freddie Mercury's sometimes feminine falsetto vocals, famously collaborating with Bowie on 'Under Pressure' in 1981.

RELATED TOPICS
See also
PUNK & NEW WAVE
page 46

FOLLOWERS OF FASHION
page 76

DAVID BOWIE
page 146

3-SECOND BIOGRAPHIES
LOU REED
1942–2013
Vocalist with pioneering band the Velvet Underground, founding father of glam rock

BRYAN FERRY
1945–
Singer, songwriter, pianist and leader of Roxy Music

MARC BOLAN
1947–77
Pioneer glam singer, songwriter and guitarist of T. Rex

30-SECOND TEXT
Paul Kingsbury

Glam rock was about independence from gender norms, dress codes and pretentious musical jams.

3-SECOND LICK
A reaction to rock's self-importance, glam rock was both a fashion statement and a musical genre that flowered in the first half of the 1970s.

3-MINUTE JAM
Bowie was glam rock's lynchpin and leading light. He set the standard in glam fashion with sexually provocative, androgynous stage wear designed by Kansai Yamamoto. Musically, he also produced and arranged successful albums for fellow glam stars Iggy Pop, Lou Reed and Mott the Hoople, the latter scoring a breakthrough hit with the Bowie song 'All the Young Dudes'.

AOR ROCK
the 30-second rock

With ground-breaking LPs like *Revolver* and *Sgt. Pepper's Lonely Hearts Club Band*, the Beatles forever redefined the rock album as an artistic statement, with each track meant to be significant. In response, FM radio in the US began programming album cuts, leaving singles to the AM stations. For UK audiences, Radio Luxembourg had a similar album focus in its late-night programming. It was the beginning of AOR – album-oriented rock radio. AOR attracted the hip listeners of the 1970s, and rewarded bands that dared to stretch out with epic tracks. Led Zeppelin's 'Stairway to Heaven', and Lynyrd Skynyrd's 'Free Bird' for instance, became immortal rock anthems thanks to heavy AOR airplay. Although originally intended as free-form, wide-open broadcasting, by the mid-1970s AOR radio had coalesced around white, pop-melodic, guitar-based rock, embodied by the Eagles, the Doobie Brothers, Fleetwood Mac, Boston, Supertramp, Styx, Kansas, Foreigner, Journey and REO Speedwagon. What began as a trailblazing radio format eventually became a badge of dishonour, signifying bland, middle-of-the-road music. To be called an AOR band nowadays is to be dismissed as stodgy and safe. But weep not for AOR – the music lives on in the 'Classic Rock' format of many radio stations today.

RELATED TOPICS
See also
THE SINGLE
page 58

THE ALBUM
page 60

BUBBLEGUM
page 110

THE BEATLES: *REVOLVER*
page 120

3-SECOND BIOGRAPHIES
TOM DONAHUE
1928–75
DJ who pioneered the AOR radio format in 1967 in San Francisco

LEE ABRAMS
1952–
Radio executive who widely popularized the AOR radio format, starting in 1971 in North Carolina

30-SECOND TEXT
Paul Kingsbury

'AOR' is now code for stodgy and safe rock. But once upon a time it signified a window onto fresh, new sounds.

3-SECOND LICK
AOR began as an innovative radio format focusing on album cuts, but the term eventually came to describe glossy, commercial rock.

3-MINUTE JAM
The bands that tend to be lumped together as AOR, such as the Eagles, Foreigner, Boston and Journey, represent a range of styles from LA country rock to prog rock lite. So what do they have in common? A 1970s–80s heyday, and massive commercial success; guitar-driven musical arrangements scrubbed of rough edges; high-pitched vocals; melodic, hummable tunes which can be up-tempo and energized, but in a soothing rather than an abrasive way. In short, lounge chair rock.

23 September 1949
Born in Freehold,
New Jersey

1965
Plays 'British Invasion'
hits in a covers band

1971
Assembles the group that
will become the E Street
Band, and is nicknamed
The Boss

1973
Releases his first album,
*Greetings from Asbury
Park, N.J.*

1974
Journalist Jon Landau
sees Springsteen perform
and writes, 'I saw rock
and roll's future and its
name is Bruce Springsteen'

1978
Following managerial
problems, Springsteen
releases first album for
three years, *Darkness on
the Edge of Town*

1984
President Reagan
mistakes 'Born in the
USA' for a patriotic
anthem

1994
Wins Oscar for title song
from *Philadelphia*
starring Tom Hanks and
Denzel Washington

2002
Releases *The Rising*,
his response to the
9/11 attacks

2006
Releases *We Shall
Overcome*, a tribute
album to Pete Seeger

2012
After releasing *Wrecking
Ball*, Springsteen begins
18-month world tour

2016
His autobiography, *Born
to Run*, is a worldwide
bestseller

BRUCE SPRINGSTEEN

Bruce Frederick Springsteen was born on 23 September 1949 in Freehold, New Jersey. He had a difficult childhood, torn between a supportive mother and a critical father who resented his presence. An Italian-American, he found it difficult to accept the tenets of Catholicism, an issue which would permeate his lyrics. Buying a guitar for $18 when he was 15, he started playing 'British Invasion' hits, and was soon leading his own band in Asbury Park while living in an attic above a surfboard factory.

Signed to Columbia by John Hammond, his first album, made with the E Street Band, *Greetings From Asbury Park, N. J.*, was followed by *The Wild, the Innocent & the E Street Shuffle* (both 1973). He was hailed as the new Dylan, but while Dylan was primarily a social commentator, Springsteen identified with blue-collar America. In 1975 he hit the big-time with the title song and album, *Born to Run*. However, believing that he was being exploited, he sued his manager, Mike Appel, and Jon Landau took over in 1977, the year before *Darkness on the Edge of Town*.

Dressed in undershirt and jeans, Springsteen's hard-rocking, sweat-drenched live performances stretched to four hours with the repertoire varying from night to night. 'Born in the USA' (1984) is a bitter song about unemployment, but audiences punch the sky when he sings it. The E Street Band has included Steve Van Zandt and Nils Lofgren (guitars) and Clarence Clemons (saxophone), although Springsteen worked without them for many years. He has also made numerous guest appearances, and written for other performers (Pointer Sisters, Patti Smith, Gary 'US' Bonds).

In 1985 he married model Julianne Phillips, but by *Tunnel of Love* (1987), it was evident that things were not going well. In 1990 he started a family with band member Patti Scialfa, and they married the following year. He reunited with the E Street Band for *The Rising* in 2002, Springsteen's response to the 9/11 attacks.

A prolific singer-songwriter with a strong conscience, Bruce Springsteen is *the* key figure in stadium rock. In 2017 he played the farewell concert for President Barack Obama.

Spencer Leigh

BRITPOP

the 30-second rock

Britpop was presented as the antithesis of grunge. In contrast to the dark, minor chord thrashings of Nirvana and Soundgarden, Britpop was upbeat, brash and optimistic, the bands sporting colourful, flashy clothes instead of earth-toned plaid flannel shirts. Britpop was heavily influenced not only by the music of the 1960s — the Beatles, The Kinks and The Who among the most frequently cited — but also by its visual elements, specifically the Union Jack, which was much featured in 1960s mod culture, and now revived as a symbol of 'Cool Britannia' (itself an updating of the slogan 'Swinging London'). Blur, Suede, Pulp and Oasis were the best known of the Britpop acts; at the height of the movement, Blur and Oasis were the focus of a media-driven 'British Heavyweight Championship', when their singles, 'Country House' and 'Roll With It' respectively, were released on the same date, 14 August 1995 (Blur won, outselling Oasis by some 60,000 copies). The term didn't only apply to music; young, modern British artists, designers and filmmakers were also tagged with the label; even Prime Minister Tony Blair and his New Labour Party aligned themselves with the 'Cool Britannia' spirit. But by the end of the decade, Britpop was over, with most of the leading bands breaking up.

3-SECOND LICK
As grunge was rising to prominence in the USA, Britpop emerged at the same time, championing a very different musical style, and a distinctly British voice.

3-MINUTE JAM
Oasis was the only Britpop band to enjoy substantial success on both sides of the Atlantic – despite the continual arguments between founding members Liam and Noel Gallagher, which plagued a number of their US performances. The singles 'Wonderwall' and 'Champagne Supernova' topped the US charts, a feat no other Britpop act matched. Oasis also toured the USA more extensively than other acts, a necessity to gain an audience in such a large country.

RELATED TOPICS
See also
BEAT, BLUES & FOLK ROCK
page 38

MANCHESTER
page 142

3-SECOND BIOGRAPHIES
JARVIS COCKER
1963–
Lead vocalist and guitarist with Pulp, followed by solo career

NOEL GALLAGHER
1967–
Guitarist, vocalist and principal songwriter with Oasis, later fronted High Flying Birds

DAMON ALBARN
1968–
Lead singer of Blur, later co-founder of 'virtual' band Gorillaz

30-SECOND TEXT
Gillian G. Gaar

Blur (left) vs Oasis (right) was Britpop's biggest feud.

BUBBLEGUM

the 30-second rock

In 1968 Neil Bogart of Buddah Records saw a marketing opportunity: rock music was becoming an art form, with the pre-teens being left behind. Following a US number one with the Lemon Pipers' 'Green Tambourine', he commissioned the producers Jerry Kasenetz and Jeff Katz to write catchy, uncomplicated records aimed at 11-year-olds. With Joey Levine as the adenoidal lead singer, they created hits for the 1910 Fruitgum Company ('Simon Says', '1, 2, 3, Red Light'), Ohio Express ('Yummy Yummy Yummy', 'Chewy Chewy') and even the narcissistic Kasenetz-Katz Singing Orchestral Circus ('Quick Joey Small'). The music press derided the product as 'bubblegum', the term being applied to other performers seeking similar success. The most enduring records have been Tommy Roe's 'Dizzy' and the Archies' 'Sugar, Sugar', both US chart toppers in 1969, the latter created for a TV cartoon series. In the UK, several acts (Edison Lighthouse, the Pipkins, the Tremeloes) had bubblegum hits. Bubblegum can be traced back to Beatles' records ('Eight Days a Week', 'Yellow Submarine'), early Monkees' songs, Bobby Vee's 'Rubber Ball' and the nursery-rhyme pop of Freddie and the Dreamers. Its influence can be seen in the Jackson 5, the Bay City Rollers and *The Partridge Family*, and the concept of assembly-line pop has never gone away.

RELATED TOPICS
See also
BEAT, BLUES & FOLK ROCK
page 38

THE SINGLE
page 58

PRODUCERS
page 62

GLAM ROCK
page 102

3-SECOND BIOGRAPHIES
TOMMY ROE
1942–
Wrote and sang 1969 hit 'Dizzy'

JERRY KASENETZ & JEFF KATZ
both 1943–
Songwriting and production team

30-SECOND TEXT
Spencer Leigh

Bubblegum pop stars, clockwise from top: Bobby Vee, Bay City Rollers, Freddie Garrity (of Freddie and the Dreamers) and David Cassidy (star of The Partridge Family).

3-SECOND LICK
Bubblegum is simple, catchy, dance-oriented pop of the late 1960s, epitomized in the Archies' 'Sugar, Sugar' and Tommy Roe's 'Dizzy'.

3-MINUTE JAM
Jerry Kasenetz and Jeff Katz of Super K Productions created bubblegum pop: simple, catchy records with strong hooks and infectious dance beats. Bubblegum represented a time when session singers came into their own – Joey Levine with the 1910 Fruitgum Company and Ohio Express, Ron Dante with the Archies and Tony Burrows with Edison Lighthouse and the Pipkins. It is criticized as lightweight and cynical, a judgement that could be levelled at much other popular music.

CLASSIC RECORDS

acoustic Pertaining to sound (as in the acoustic quality of a venue, for instance). More specifically, meaning unamplified, as in an acoustic non-electric guitar.

avant-garde Literally, from the French for 'vanguard'. Refers to new and experimental ideas in the arts, including music; also describes those artists, writers or musicians working in such areas.

beat poetry The 'beat generation' writers of the mid-1950s, most famously Allen Ginsberg (*Howl*, 1956) and Jack Kerouac (*On the Road*, 1957), inspired a free-form 'stream of consciousness' style of lyric writing in the work of a number of rock songwriters including Bob Dylan, John Lennon and Tom Waits.

double LP A vinyl album consisting of two discs, to accommodate up to twice the normal playing time, usually packaged in a double 'gatefold' sleeve.

Euro Disco Electronic dance music that evolved in Europe during the late 1970s, usually distinguished by the injection of new wave, pop and rock influences into a disco-dance context.

grunge Specifically describing the alternative rock of 1990s (mainly) Seattle bands including Nirvana, Soundgarden and Pearl Jam, and similar groups who followed in their wake.

guitar break A short guitar solo, punctuating a vocal or instrumental recording or live performance.

hook A catchy chorus, repeated instrumental figure, or bridge passage between verses, which almost literally 'hooks' the listener into a pop song.

looping The use of short sections of music (or other sound) repeated continuously, to get a particular (often 'hypnotic') effect. The term originates from tape looping, but now a loop can be created by many music technologies including digital samplers, drum machines, synthesizers and so on.

Pop Art Art movement that flourished during the 1950s and 1960s, inspired by – and utilizing – the visual language of comic books, newspapers and advertising. In the United States the leading names included Jasper Johns, Roy Lichtenstein and Andy Warhol, while in the UK the movement was pioneered by Eduardo Paolozzi, Richard Hamilton (who went on to design the Beatles' 'White Album' cover), David Hockney and Peter Blake (designer of *Sgt. Pepper*, among several album covers).

platinum sales In the UK, a platinum disc is awarded to albums certified to have sold 300,000 copies, and to singles selling 600,000 copies. In the USA, the award applies to any album or single having sold a million copies. The sales of an album that sells two million in the US, for example, will be said to be 'double platinum' or 'multi platinum'. Further differing thresholds apply in other territories. Since 2013, on-demand audio and video streaming of music has also been taken into account in calculating the sales figures of music.

power chord An informal name for a chord consisting of the root note and the fifth note in a particular key, vigorously played on an electric guitar, and often with an element of distortion applied. Power chords are used to great effect in many forms of rock, and are a particular feature of punk and heavy metal.

psychedelic Pertaining to the effects of hallucinogenic drugs (primarily LSD), and describing music, art and literature inspired by their use.

session musician A freelance professional musician, hired (often on a session-by-session basis) to contribute to studio recordings. May also be employed to back vocalists or augment regular groups in a live concert capacity. A number of notable session musicians, for instance Led Zeppelin's Jimmy Page, and keyboard player Rick Wakeman, rose from the ranks of studio work to become star performers in their own right – as did the house band at Stax Records in Memphis, when they had their 1962 hit 'Green Onions' as Booker T. & the M.G.s.

ELVIS PRESLEY
'HEARTBREAK HOTEL'

the 30-second rock

3-SECOND LICK
Elvis Presley's 1956 single was his greatest achievement: a confident vocal, a suicidal song, sparse but perfect musicianship and, naturally, looks to die for.

3-MINUTE JAM
Although 'Heartbreak Hotel' sounds so familiar today, it could have come from outer space in 1956, an example of how well an alien sound has been embraced by our culture. It was a major US hit on the pop, country and R&B charts, an indication of rock 'n' roll's cultural roots. Welcome to the echo chamber, and popular music would never be the same again.

In August 1955, aspiring writer Alvin Krolik was killed while robbing a liquor store in El Paso, Texas. He left behind an unpublished memoir with the words, 'This is the story of someone who walks a lonely street.' Songwriters Mae Boren Axton and Tommy Durden read about him, and wrote 'Heartbreak Hotel' within 30 minutes. When Axton played it to Elvis Presley, the singer was moving from Sun Records to RCA, and his new producer, Steve Sholes, saw the song's potential. Colonel Parker, Elvis's astute manager, negotiated a writing credit for him. The session in January 1956 featured Scotty Moore's emphatic guitar break, Bill Black's bass and Floyd Cramer's piano. Elvis immersed himself into the lyric, effectively method acting, a performance reminiscent of Johnnie Ray's sensational sob-song 'Cry' (1951). It was only the second rock 'n' roll number one, but it was markedly different from the first, Bill Haley's dance tune 'Rock Around the Clock' (1955). It topped the US charts for eight weeks, and Presley became the most controversial entertainer in America, signifying a parting of the ways between the adult and teenage markets. The record was immediately influential. Its excessive echo was copied by Gene Vincent for his hit 'Be-Bop-A-Lula', and parodied by the humourist Stan Freberg, both within months of its release.

RELATED TOPICS
See also
ELVIS PRESLEY
page 26

THE FIRST ROCK 'N' ROLL
RECORD
page 28

CLASSIC ROCK 'N' ROLL
page 36

THE SINGLE
page 58

3-SECOND BIOGRAPHIES
STEVE SHOLES
1911–68
Record executive who signed Elvis to RCA Records, produced most of his 1950s hit singles

MAE BOREN AXTON
1914–97
Rock 'n' roll and country songwriter

SCOTTY MOORE
1931–2016
Much-emulated lead guitarist

30-SECOND TEXT
Spencer Leigh

Real-life drama inspired 'Heartbreak Hotel', Elvis Presley's first international hit.

BOB DYLAN
BRINGING IT ALL BACK HOME

the 30-second rock

This was the fifth album from
the messianic singer-songwriter, also his first to
feature electric instrumentation, leading to cries
of 'sell-out' from diehard fans, who had come
to see him as the spokesman of the 1960s.
Bringing It All Back Home was recorded in a
three-day burst in January 1965. From the cover
in, this marked the emergence of a 'new Dylan'
– the denim-clad folk protestor replaced by a
fashionable streetwise dandy. The title was a
homage to British groups like the Beatles and
Rolling Stones, who were reminding American
audiences of their own musical heritage. The
11-track album was split: side one was effectively
rock 'n' roll, with a nod to electric Chicago blues.
Side two was predominantly 'folk', with Dylan
accompanying himself on acoustic guitar
and harmonica. The album opened with the
clarion call 'Subterranean Homesick Blues',
acknowledging Chuck Berry's 'Too Much Monkey
Business' (1956). There was frivolity ('Bob Dylan's
115th Dream'), while lyrically there was none of
his earlier overt protest. The album also featured
searing love songs such as 'She Belongs to Me'.
The four acoustic songs are counted as some
of Dylan's best ever, notably the majestic 'Mr.
Tambourine Man' and the poignant, concluding
'It's All Over Now Baby Blue', which draws a line
under a crucial period of Dylan's career.

3-SECOND LICK
The landmark fifth album
from Dylan, which on its
release alienated his folk
following with its overt
rock instrumentation, but
lyrically saw him reaching
new heights.

3-MINUTE JAM
Only the Beatles matched
the changes Bob Dylan
underwent during the
turbulent years of 1965 and
1966. Dylan's three albums
of the period (*Bringing It
All Back Home*, *Highway 61
Revisited* and *Blonde on
Blonde*, rock's first double
LP) rebuilt the musical
landscape. *Bringing It All
Back Home* was key in
reconnecting with Dylan's
original love of rock 'n' roll,
while taking pop lyricism
to a new dimension.

RELATED TOPICS
See also
BEAT, BLUES & FOLK ROCK
page 38

BOB DYLAN
page 86

3-SECOND BIOGRAPHIES
ALLEN GINSBERG
1926–97
'Beat' poet pictured on the
album's back sleeve, whose
work influenced Dylan

TOM WILSON
1931–78
Producer of *The Times They
Are a-Changin'* (1964), *Another
Side of Bob Dylan* (1964) and
Bringing It All Back Home

BRUCE LANGHORNE
1938–2017
Session guitarist, whose
enormous African tambourine
Dylan cited as an influence on
'Mr. Tambourine Man'

30-SECOND TEXT
Patrick Humphries

*A shady, cool-looking
Dylan in the CBS
studios about to
electrify the world.*

THE BEATLES
REVOLVER

the 30-second rock

RELATED TOPICS
See also
BEAT, BLUES & FOLK ROCK
page 38

THE BEATLES
page 40

PRODUCERS
page 62

SONGWRITERS
page 66

3-SECOND LICK
Although they had revolutionized rock music with their six previous long-players, *Revolver* remains the most radical of all the Beatles' albums.

3-MINUTE JAM
Not only do the 14 tracks display an astonishing variety of styles and influences, but the musical and technical innovations on *Revolver* also helped change the face of rock forever. Most of the songs were born in individual Beatles' home studios, before being developed with producer George Martin at Abbey Road. Although their previous album *Rubber Soul* was certainly innovative, it had a common feel throughout, while on *Revolver* no two tracks were at all similar.

From George Harrison's protest about the taxman taking his money, to the surreal closure of John Lennon's mystical lyrics on 'Tomorrow Never Knows', track by track the Beatles' 1966 classic *Revolver* never ceases to surprise. Harrison makes his first recorded statement in his exploration of Indian music on 'Love You To', playing with instrumentalists from the sub-continent. McCartney's lyricism excels in the ballads 'For No One', 'Here There and Everywhere' (inspired by the Beach Boys' 'God Only Knows') and the emotive loneliness of 'Eleanor Rigby', which one critic declared was pop music's 'coming of age'. There's a nod to the jazz-inflected music of Motown with 'Got to Get You into My Life', while the joyful optimism of 'Good Day Sunshine' and Lennon's 'I'm Only Sleeping' and 'Tomorrow Never Knows' are early examples of 'psychedelic' music. Experimentation abounds: most obviously on 'Tomorrow Never Knows' with its tape loop effects, synthesized vocals and reversed guitar parts, but also on Lennon's dream-like 'I'm Only Sleeping' with Harrison's backward-recorded guitar solo. And sound effects of every kind are brought to bear on 'Yellow Submarine', the ultimate modern nursery rhyme; amid the audacious experiments, an example of the essential populism that was at the heart of the Beatles' success.

3-SECOND BIOGRAPHIES
GEORGE MARTIN
1926–2016
The Beatles' producer and the prime architect of their recorded output

KLAUS VOORMAN
1938–
Illustrator, designed the cover for *Revolver*. A friend of the Beatles since their days in Hamburg, also bass player, guitarist and record producer

30-SECOND TEXT
Mike Evans

The Beatles were at the peak of their creativity when Revolver *was released in August 1966.*

THE VELVET UNDERGROUND
THE VELVET UNDERGROUND & NICO

the 30-second rock

Undeniably one of the most influential albums ever made, the LP sold poorly on its initial release in 1967. But as Brian Eno later wrote, 'The first Velvet Underground album only sold 10,000 copies, but everyone who bought it formed a band!' Artist Andy Warhol had been alerted to the band and is listed as the producer of their debut. The Velvets were formed around the core of singer-songwriter Lou Reed and multi-instrumentalist John Cale. Ice-cool model Nico provided an additional focal point. The sheer relentless menace of the Velvet Underground was apparent on the drug paeans 'I'm Waiting For the Man' and 'Heroin'. Sado-masochism was tackled on 'Venus in Furs'. The atonal, feedback-fuelled 'Black Angel's Death Song' and 'European Son' guaranteed minimum airplay. That musical brutality was balanced by the Nico-led ballads 'Femme Fatale' and 'All Tomorrow's Parties'. *The Velvet Underground & Nico* was turned down by a number of major labels, and on its eventual release, critics and fans were appalled by the bleakness of its vision, at odds with the peace and love vibes then emanating from San Francisco. Among those immediately influenced by the album was David Bowie, while later fans included Joy Division, Siouxsie and the Banshees, and the Jesus and Mary Chain.

3-SECOND LICK
Bleak and musically challenging, this album paved the way for everyone from David Bowie to U2 to explore the possibilities of what rock could accomplish.

3-MINUTE JAM
After over half a century since its initial release in 1967, *The Velvet Underground & Nico* still divides opinion. Its defenders argue that the album was instrumental in introducing various avant-garde concepts into the pop mainstream, while critics still rail against its seeming monotony, and bleak lyrical pessimism. All agree, however, that the record remains one of just a handful of albums that genuinely influenced the future direction of rock music.

RELATED TOPICS
See also
PUNK & NEW WAVE
page 46

ELECTRO-ROCK
page 48

3-SECOND BIOGRAPHIES
ANDY WARHOL
1928–87
Pop artist. His hands-on role as producer is disputed, but it was undeniably Warhol who initially encouraged the band

LOU REED
1942–2013
Took rock to extremes, but also contributed much-loved hits 'Walk on the Wild Side' and 'Perfect Day'

JOHN CALE
1942–
At odds with Reed during the band's short career, Cale continues to challenge expectations in his musical odyssey

30-SECOND TEXT
Patrick Humphries

Warhol's famous banana from the band's debut album cover.

27 November 1942
Born Johnny Allen
Hendrix in Seattle,
Washington

1961
Enlists as army
paratrooper with 101st
Airborne Division, but
discharged the following
year after injury

1965
Cuts his teeth as guitarist
performing with the Isley
Brothers, Little Richard
and Curtis Knight

1966
Discovered playing in
Greenwich Village by the
Animals' Chas Chandler,
who persuades Hendrix
to travel to London

1967
'Hey Joe' gives the Jimi
Hendrix Experience its
first hit, followed by
'Purple Haze' and 'The
Wind Cries Mary'; also
sees release of debut LP,
and ground-breaking
appearance at Monterey
Pop Festival

1968
Extensive tours of
America. Release of
self-produced double LP,
Electric Ladyland, which
includes 'All Along the
Watchtower' and
'Voodoo Chile'. Splits
with manager Chandler

1969
Jimi Hendrix Experience
split. Hendrix plays
Woodstock Festival, and
debuts Band of Gypsys
in New York on New
Year's Eve

1970
Opens Electric Ladyland
studio; plays Isle of
Wight Festival

18 September 1970
Found dead in London,
aged 27

JIMI HENDRIX

Revered as rock's greatest

guitarist, Jimi Hendrix only released four albums in his lifetime. A career as a road guitarist in America following his discharge from army service did little to showcase his abilities. Discovery by the Animals' Chas Chandler in New York led to Hendrix settling in London in late 1966. It was the extraordinary fluency of his playing which so impressed peers like Jeff Beck, Eric Clapton and Pete Townshend. Already steeped in blues, Hendrix's work soon embraced jazz and pop. Too often, though, the quality of his playing was overshadowed by the flamboyance of his live performances – famously playing behind his head or setting fire to his guitar.

Bassist Noel Redding and drummer Mitch Mitchell proved perfect bandmates for the Jimi Hendrix Experience, who were soon enjoying early chart hits like 'Hey Joe' and the Bob Dylan-influenced 'The Wind Cries Mary'. Hendrix's version of 'All Along the Watchtower' has long been hailed as the best-ever Dylan cover. 'Purple Haze' marked the emergence of a heavier, more distinctive Hendrix sound, and he soon became known for his lengthy improvisations, which were better suited to the concert stage. Early tours found him incongruously sharing bills with Engelbert Humperdinck and The Monkees. By 1968 he was headlining tours of his native America, and his performance of 'The Star-Spangled Banner' at Woodstock in 1969 became the stuff of legend. Hendrix could seemingly play anything – pop, R&B, blues, hard rock, jazz – while embracing the latest studio technology. He was only truly happy with the double *Electric Ladyland* album, which he 'produced and directed', its release delayed as he agonized over the final sequencing. Hendrix made it all seem so effortless, whether acoustic blues or electrifying rock. His playing even impressed the notoriously hard to please jazz maestro Miles Davis, who expressed interest in their recording together.

After splitting with Chandler, Hendrix's career became mired in litigation and political trauma. His tragically early death robbed rock of one of its true originals, and we can only speculate where he would have taken his music had he lived. At least a dozen posthumous studio albums have appeared since 1970, plus innumerable live sets. In 1997, in recognition of his standing, English Heritage unveiled its first blue plaque to a rock musician, marking the flat he occupied in London.

Patrick Humphries

BLONDIE
PARALLEL LINES

the 30-second rock

3-SECOND LICK
The breakthrough album by new wave act Blondie, fuelled by the international smash hit 'Heart of Glass'.

3-MINUTE JAM
'Heart of Glass', Blondie's most famous song, dated back to the earliest days of the group, when it was known as 'Once I Had a Love'. They'd previously tried performing it in various styles (Harry recalled ballad and reggae versions), finally settling on a percussive style influenced by American disco as well as 'Euro Disco', an electronic music style popularized by producers like Giorgio Moroder. It was the disco beat that gave the song its percussive 'hook'.

After releasing two albums of new wave-infused power pop to moderate success, the release of *Parallel Lines* finally kicked opened the doors for Blondie. The best-known track would be the disco-flavoured 'Heart of Glass' (co-written by Blondie's lead singer, Deborah Harry, and the band's guitarist, Chris Stein), which topped the charts in eight different countries and became the band's signature song. But the rest of the album revealed that the group was far more than just a disco act. *Parallel Lines* had much diversity: 'Sunday Girl' harkened back to the girl group era of the early 1960s; the fuzzy tones of 'Fade Away and Radiate' had a touch of psychedelia; 'Hanging on the Telephone' and 'One Way or Another' were bristling slices of power pop; and there was a high-spirited rock 'n' roll cover of Buddy Holly's 'I'm Gonna Love You Too'. Harry's cool, clear vocals exuded an ironic detachment; this was a band that delivered their songs with a wink. *Parallel Lines* also marked the first time producer Mike Chapman (who'd previously produced the Sweet, Mud and Suzi Quatro) worked with the group, and he gave the album a commercial sheen that Blondie's first two albums had lacked (he continued working with the band through 1982). The album topped the UK charts, and reached number six in the USA.

RELATED TOPICS
See also
PUNK & NEW WAVE
page 46

WOMEN IN ROCK
page 82

GIRL GROUPS
page 98

3-SECOND BIOGRAPHIES
DEBORAH HARRY
1945–
Founding member and lead singer of Blondie, solo artist and actress

MIKE CHAPMAN
1947–
Songwriter and producer who worked with Sweet, Suzi Quatro, Mud, Blondie and The Knack

CHRIS STEIN
1950–
Founding member and guitarist of Blondie

30-SECOND TEXT
Gillian G. Gaar

Blondie took new wave firmly into the mainstream with the success of Parallel Lines *and 'Heart of Glass'.*

NIRVANA
NEVERMIND

the 30-second rock

3-SECOND LICK
With their second album, Nirvana crafted the definitive grunge sound – a melodic amalgam of punk and metal that was incredibly commercial, but no sell-out.

3-MINUTE JAM
Nirvana put Seattle, Washington, on the map, musically speaking. There had been an active local rock scene there since the 1980s, but Nirvana's incredible commercial success popularized local slacker fashions, and drew attention to fellow grunge bands in the area, such as Pearl Jam, Soundgarden, Mudhoney and Alice in Chains.

Nirvana, a Seattle-based trio, changed the game for alt-rock with the release of *Nevermind* in September 1991. Their aggressive yet hook-filled metal-punk blend, dubbed 'grunge', took the music world by storm and proved alt-rock could sell. No one expected it. Their first album, *Bleach*, sold only 40,000 copies. But lead singer, guitarist and songwriter Kurt Cobain was a fiercely creative and intelligent musician. Drawing on the mainstream metal of Led Zeppelin and Black Sabbath, and the alt-rock of Sonic Youth, the Pixies and the Melvins, Cobain forged a sound that alternated quiet verse passages with loud, aggressive choruses, a technique borrowed from the Pixies. Tracks like 'Smells Like Teen Spirit', 'Lithium' and 'In Bloom' go from a conspiratorial murmur to an angry roar and back again, driven by Cobain's impassioned vocals and slashing power chords, the gripping traction of Krist Novoselic's bass and Dave Grohl's powerful yet precise drumming. Label execs deemed producer Butch Vig's proposed mix of the album too murky, so producer-engineer Andy Wallace remixed it for a brighter, more detailed sound. It worked. To date *Nevermind* has been certified for sales of over 10 million copies. Cobain, a heroin addict, committed suicide on 5 April 1994. Grohl moved on to lead the alt-rock band Foo Fighters in 1995.

RELATED TOPICS
See also
HEAVY METAL
page 44

PUNK & NEW WAVE
page 46

INDIE & ALT-ROCK
page 50

SEATTLE
page 140

3-SECOND BIOGRAPHIES
KRIST NOVOSELIC
1965–
Singer, bassist for Nirvana, Sweet 75, Eyes Adrift and Giants in the Trees

KURT COBAIN
1967–94
Singer, songwriter and guitarist

DAVE GROHL
1969–
Drummer for Nirvana, and singer, songwriter and guitarist for Foo Fighters

30-SECOND TEXT
Paul Kingsbury

Nirvana proved with their fierce, melodic album that alt-rock could sell millions.

THE WHITE STRIPES
THE WHITE STRIPES

the 30-second rock

Consider the sheer audacity.

They were a two-person band from Detroit, a young man and woman – brother and sister they claimed at first, though it was later revealed they were married – doing blues-based rock with just drums and guitar, or occasionally piano. They confined their stage costuming and album artwork strictly to three colours: red, white and black. Their sound was raw, lo-fi and minimalist. It was also totally assured and riveting. All 17 tracks on their debut album blaze with a fierce intelligence behind the rock 'n' roll thunder. Who were these cocksure kids? Jack White was a furniture upholstery worker from Detroit, a recent convert to the blues by way of Bob Dylan and Led Zeppelin. He revered country blues artists like Robert Johnson, Son House and Blind Willie McTell – he dedicated the album to House. Meg was a gifted novice on drums. Fourteen tracks were originals, complemented by self-assured reworkings of Johnson's 'Stop Breaking Down', Dylan's 'One More Cup of Coffee' and the jazz-blues standard 'St. James Infirmary'. Other standouts include acoustic ballad 'Sugar Never Tasted So Good', and the chugging electric strutter 'Astro'. 'I still feel we've never topped our first album,' Jack White has said. 'It's the most raw, the most powerful and the most Detroit-sounding record we've made.'

3-SECOND LICK
Though unheralded upon its 1999 release, the debut album of The White Stripes signalled Jack White's intention to refashion blues rock in bold new ways.

3-MINUTE JAM
The White Stripes didn't exactly conquer the world with their 1999 album debut on the independent label Sympathy for the Record Industry, and *Rolling Stone* magazine did not even review it. There were no hit singles among its 17 tracks, but the rock DNA was there. By their fourth album, *Elephant*, in 2003, The White Stripes achieved platinum sales, and they also won two Grammy Awards.

RELATED TOPICS
See also
COUNTRY BLUES
page 16

HEAVY METAL
page 44

PUNK & NEW WAVE,
page 46

INDIE & ALT-ROCK
page 50

DETROIT
page 138

3-SECOND BIOGRAPHIES
MEG WHITE
1974–
Drummer and singer for The White Stripes

JACK WHITE
1975–
Singer, musician, songwriter, producer and creative force behind The White Stripes, the Raconteurs, the Dead Weather and Third Man Records

30-SECOND TEXT
Paul Kingsbury

The White Stripes showed that two musicians could create a 'wall of sound'.

AMY WINEHOUSE
BACK TO BLACK

the 30-second rock

Amy Winehouse was a working-class girl from north London, the child of a broken home. She struggled with depression, alcohol and drug abuse, and bulimia, but she had talent to burn and exquisite musical taste. Her musical idols were jazzy pop singers: Dinah Washington, Sarah Vaughan and Tony Bennett. Yet she also loved R&B and hip-hop. Her supple, street-smart singing effortlessly blended all those styles. Her first album was *Frank* (2003), a collection of risqué personal vignettes largely written by Winehouse and set to breezy, jazz-inflected grooves. *Back to Black* tightened the focus considerably. Working with producers Mark Ronson and Salaam Remi, and the Dap-Kings retro-soul band, she created an album that recalled classic girl groups and 1960s soul, yet sounded completely of the moment. She wrote or co-wrote all ten tracks, inspired by the pain of her breakup with boyfriend Blake Fielder. The tough-talking but irresistible 'Rehab' became a worldwide hit. The album won her five Grammy Awards, a Brit Award for Best British Female Artist and two Ivor Novello songwriting awards. She seemed on her way to even greater achievements. But she was unable to overcome her addictions. She made her last recording in March 2011, a duet with Tony Bennett. She died of alcohol poisoning just four months later.

3-SECOND LICK
Reeling from a breakup, Amy Winehouse poured her pain into the album of a lifetime, a hip homage to girl groups and classic R&B.

3-MINUTE JAM
Winehouse and her producers went to great lengths to get an authentic 1960s vibe for *Back to Black*. They sampled the 1966 R&B single by the Icemen '(My Girl) She's a Fox' for 'He Can Only Hold Her', and recreated the soaring Motown arrangement of 'Ain't No Mountain High Enough' (released in 1967 by Marvin Gaye and Tammi Terrell) for 'Tears Dry on Their Own'.

RELATED TOPICS
See also
WOMEN IN ROCK
page 82

GIRL GROUPS
page 98

MOTOWN
page 100

3-SECOND BIOGRAPHIES
SALAAM REMI
1972–
R&B and hip-hop producer, worked with Amy Winehouse, Nas, Fugees, Alicia Keys and many others

MARK RONSON
1975–
DJ, songwriter and record producer for Adele, Bruno Mars, Christine Aguilera and Lady Gaga

AMY WINEHOUSE
1983–2011
Singer, songwriter and guitarist

30-SECOND TEXT
Paul Kingsbury

Amy Winehouse blended classic R&B and girl group sounds with streetwise lyrics to stunning effect.

ROCKIN' AROUND THE WORLD

ROCKIN' AROUND THE WORLD
GLOSSARY

AKB48 A multi-team girl group of over 130 members, named after the Akihabara (or 'Akiba') district of Tokyo, where their theatre is located. Formed in 2005 by Yasushi Akimoto, the 'idol you can meet' concept involves teams performing on a rotating basis at the theatre, or at various venues simultaneously.

avant-garde Literally, from the French for 'vanguard'. Refers to new and experimental ideas in the arts, including music; also describes those artists, writers or musicians working in such areas.

Cold War Name given to the political and military stand-off between the Western powers and Eastern-bloc Communist countries, that lasted from the late 1940s until the collapse of the Soviet Union in 1991.

funk Originating in the mid-1960s with the music of James Brown, funk was a 1970s mixture of African-American soul music, R&B and jazz, with the previous emphasis on melody giving way to insistent drum and bass rhythms. At the same time funk utilized the complex extended harmonies found in bebop jazz, but usually pared down to a repeated single chord for a driving rhythmic feel.

J-pop A fusion of Western pop and rock with more traditional Japanese music that started in the early 1970s, and developed into part of the musical mainstream of Japan by the 1990s, giving Japanese rock its own distinct character.

Merseybeat A catch-all term for bands that came out of Liverpool immediately after the UK success of the Beatles in 1963, the typical line-up consisted of two guitars, bass guitar and drums. The repertoire of most groups was classic and early 1960s US rock 'n' roll and R&B, with leading exponents including the Searchers, Gerry & the Pacemakers and the Swinging Blue Jeans.

mod Mod originated as a subculture in late 1950s London, its predominantly male members being fans of modern jazz (hence the name), dressing in neat Italian-inspired suits, and often riding Italian motor scooters. In the early 1960s mods embraced the emerging R&B scene and the bands associated with it, and by the middle of the decade a whole fashion-conscious teenage sub-group, identified with rock bands like The Who and the Small Faces, was now labelled 'mod'.

Northern Soul A music and dance movement that developed in northern England in the 1970s at venues like Wigan Casino and the Mecca Ballroom in Blackpool, flourished through the 1980s and 1990s, and still has a dedicated following. Basically a revival of mod style and music, it was not a music genre as such but a reflection of dancers' and DJs' tastes, concentrated on the more obscure American soul, R&B and funk records from the 1960s and early 1970s.

rave The rave scene developed from acid house parties of the late 1980s in Chicago in the US, and initially Manchester in the UK. The early raves were large-scale gatherings, often held at unofficial or illegal venues, featuring DJs playing dance-oriented psychedelic and electronic music. The highly amplified records were usually accompanied by laser light shows and fog machines. Since then the term has come to describe the subculture centred on similar club venues, and strongly associated with the use of various recreational drugs.

Riot grrrls Underground punk feminist movement originating in the early 1990s in the American Northwest. It addresses issues like rape, domestic abuse and female empowerment, via both music and social activism.

techno Electronic dance music emanating from Detroit in the late 1980s, which fused funk, electro-rock and jazz with the Euro-electronic sounds of Kraftwerk and others.

timbre The character of a musical or vocal sound, as opposed to its tone or pitch.

Weimar Republic Refers to the German state from 1919 to the Nazi take-over in 1933.

DETROIT

the 30-second rock

RELATED TOPICS
See also
GIRL GROUPS
page 98

MOTOWN
page 100

THE WHITE STRIPES
THE WHITE STRIPES
page 130

In the pre-rock era, Detroit was home to thriving blues, jazz, R&B and gospel scenes. John Lee Hooker recorded his first hit record in Detroit in 1948, and other notable performers included Della Reese, Hank Ballard & the Midnighters and Wilson Pickett (who got his start in gospel group the Violinaires). Aretha Franklin, after starting out as a jazz singer on Columbia Records, found greater success as a soul act with Atlantic Records. Berry Gordy, Jr., an aspiring songwriter who worked on a car assembly line, launched his first record labels, Tamla (1959) and Motown (1960). In keeping with the company's slogan, 'The Sound of Young America', Gordy, an African-American, was determined that his acts should crossover from the R&B to the pop charts, with the Miracles, Mary Wells, the Supremes, the Temptations, Stevie Wonder, Martha & the Vandellas and Marvin Gaye becoming some of the label's biggest hitmakers. Post-Motown (the company permanently relocated to Los Angeles by 1972), the funk of George Clinton's Parliament-Funkadelic rose to prominence, along with rock acts like Ted Nugent and Bob Seger. More recently, Detroit-based performers have also found success in alternative rock (The White Stripes), techno (Juan Atkins) and rap (Eminem, Kid Rock).

3-SECOND LICK
The success of Detroit-based Motown Records (and its affiliated labels) gave birth to the 'Motown Sound', just one part of this city's musical history.

3-MINUTE JAM
The roots of punk rock can be found in Detroit, as well as New York City and London. The raw energy of both the MC5 and the Stooges (the latter featuring lead singer Iggy Pop) are frequently held up as examples of 'proto-punk', and acts like the Sex Pistols later covered their songs ('No Fun'). The rock magazine *CREEM*, initially based in Detroit, also covered punk well before other mainstream US music magazines.

3-SECOND BIOGRAPHIES
BERRY GORDY, JR.
1929–
Songwriter, producer, and founder of the Motown Record Corporation

ARETHA FRANKLIN
1942–
Singer-songwriter dubbed 'The Queen of Soul'

IGGY POP
1947–
Lead singer of the Stooges and solo artist, a key influence on punk rock and alt-rock

30-SECOND TEXT
Gillian G. Gaar

Detroit's rich music history includes the soul-pop of Motown, rapper Eminem and punk godfather Iggy Pop.

SEATTLE

the 30-second rock

The Pacific Northwest, and
Seattle, has produced a number of hit acts
over the years, including the Fleetwoods, the
Ventures, Heart and Kenny G. Guitar legend Jimi
Hendrix was born and raised in Seattle, though
his career breakthrough came in London. But
when Nirvana's *Nevermind* topped the US album
charts in 1992, the name of a new musical genre
entered the lexicon: grunge, a potent mash-up
of punk and heavy metal. Nirvana's success was
followed in short order by other Seattle-based
acts like Pearl Jam, Soundgarden and Alice
in Chains; the city had finally gained its own
distinct musical identity, and 'alternative rock'
became the new music industry buzzword. For
the next few years, there was a rush to sign
acts from the Pacific Northwest. Pop group
the Presidents of the United States of America
became the first post-grunge success story,
Sleater-Kinney, who emerged from the feminist-
inspired 'riot grrrl' movement, were hailed as the
'Best Band in America' by *Time* magazine, and
indie rock acts the Postal Service and the Shins
found success in the new century. Other twenty-
first-century successes include indie folk acts
Fleet Foxes, and The Head and the Heart, as
well as rapper Macklemore. But Seattle is
certainly most associated with grunge.

RELATED TOPICS
See also
INDIE & ALT-ROCK
page 50

JIMI HENDRIX
page 124

NIRVANA
NEVERMIND
page 128

3-SECOND LICK
Though home to other
stars like Jimi Hendrix, in
the 1990s Seattle became
known as the home of
'grunge', alternative rock
popularized by groups
like Nirvana.

3-MINUTE JAM
Music wasn't the only
component of grunge.
There was also a perceived
Seattle grunge 'lifestyle'
that revolved around
wearing plaid flannel shirts
and knit hats, hanging out
in one of the city's many
coffee shops (Seattle being
home to the Starbucks
coffee chain) and enjoying
local microbrews like Red
Hook and Ballard Bitter.
This is the scene depicted
in the 1992 comedy
movie *Singles*.

3-SECOND BIOGRAPHIES
BRUCE PAVITT
& JONATHAN PONEMAN
both 1959–
Co-founders of Sub Pop
Records, who released the
first records by Nirvana,
Soundgarden, the Shins and
Postal Service, among others

CHRIS CORNELL
1964–2017
Founding member, lead singer/
guitarist of Soundgarden, later
Temple of the Dog and
Audioslave

30-SECOND TEXT
Gillian G. Gaar

*The rise of grunge acts
like Nirvana finally put
Seattle on the map as
a major music mecca.*

MANCHESTER

the 30-second rock

While it may have been overshadowed by its close neighbour Liverpool during the Merseybeat era, performers from Manchester put the city on the musical map in a big way in later decades. Groups like The Hollies and Herman's Hermits hit the charts regularly during the 1960s, and the Twisted Wheel club was the centre of a thriving R&B mod scene which seeded the later semi-underground Northern Soul phenomenon. But it was a gig by the Sex Pistols at the Lower Free Trade Hall in June 1976 that got Manchester musically moving as the punk and new wave revolution clicked into gear. The Buzzcocks, Mark E. Smith with his endless re-incarnations of The Fall, two members of the seminal post-punk band Joy Division, plus one Steven Patrick Morrissey, later of The Smiths, all started here. Local TV presenter Tony Wilson was the chief catalyst with his Factory Records label and Haçienda nightclub, where in the 1980s and 1990s a new 'Madchester' scene emerged with the dance and rave sounds of bands like the Happy Mondays and The Stone Roses. Oasis kept the heritage alive in the Britpop 1990s, while Guy Garvey's Elbow led the way in the new century.

RELATED TOPICS
See also
PUNK & NEW WAVE
page 46

BRITPOP
page 108

3-SECOND LICK
'So much to answer for . . . ' sang Morrissey of his home city, a northern powerhouse of pop from the 1960s to the present day.

3-MINUTE JAM
The largest city in northern England, Manchester was not only a broadcast centre for British TV and radio (the Beatles were originally heard via local radio and TV here), but also became home to venues from small clubs like the Electric Circus and The Band on the Wall, to larger theatres like the Apollo and the 21,000-capacity Manchester Arena. The 'Northern Quarter' is the city's current creative hub, with clubs, bars and record shops.

3-SECOND BIOGRAPHIES
TONY WILSON
1950–2007
'Mr Manchester', Granada TV presenter, owner of Factory Records and the Haçienda club

IAN CURTIS
1956–80
Vocalist and songwriter with Joy Division

MORRISSEY
1959–
Singer and lyricist with The Smiths and as a solo artist

30-SECOND TEXT
Hugh Weldon

In the steps of the Sex Pistols, Manchester rose to the new wave challenge with bands like The Smiths and Joy Division leading the way.

BERLIN

the 30-second rock

By turns glam, gothic, modern and underglam, Berlin's distinctive music scene evolved out of the fractured landscape of the post-war city. Pre-war, Bertolt Brecht, Kurt Weill and Lotte Lenya had soundtracked the decadence of the Weimar Republic, but it was David Bowie's move to the Schöneberg district in 1976 that cemented the city's rock-era image – his 'Berlin trilogy' albums, and *The Idiot* which he produced for Iggy Pop, remain iconic recordings. Hansa Tonstudios in the Kreuzberg district hosted Bowie's work: other notable acts who recorded there include Depeche Mode, Killing Joke, Siouxsie and the Banshees and Nick Cave and the Bad Seeds. Cave's appearance in Wim Wenders' 1987 film *Wings of Desire* portrays the last days of the Berlin Wall; its fall in 1989 was followed by the visit of U2 to record the phenomenally successful *Achtung Baby*. In the 1990s, Berlin became a centre of the dance/techno scene, with a nightlife that led Europe in its extent and excess. Its home-based stars range from the electronic music pioneers Tangerine Dream and hard rockers Birth Control, to the pop rock of Mia, the lively latter-day punk of Die Ärzte and Sven Regener's bittersweet songs for Element of Crime.

3-SECOND LICK
The divided Cold War city produced some of the most innovative sounds of the 1970s; reunified Berlin remains one of Europe's leading music capitals.

3-MINUTE JAM
Perhaps because of its history – think of the 1972 film *Cabaret* – Berlin is more renowned for its smaller intimate venues. The Zodiak Free Arts Club was the hip centre for local musicians in the late 1960s, and SO36, immortalized in a Killing Joke song, has been a fixture since the punk days of the 1970s. But the 1,500-capacity Berghain is the go-to dance/techno club, housed in a former power station close to the old East/West border.

RELATED TOPICS
See also
ELECTRO-ROCK
page 48

DAVID BOWIE
page 146

MELBOURNE
page 148

3-SECOND BIOGRAPHIES
KLAUS SCHULZE
1947–
Electronic groundbreaker with Ash Ra Tempel, Tangerine Dream and solo

NINA HAGEN
1955–
Theatrical vocalist, the 'Godmother of Punk'

ELLEN ALLIEN
1969–
Electronic musician, music producer and founder of BPitch Control music label

30-SECOND TEXT
Hugh Weldon

1970s Berlin was a magnet for Bowie and many more, but with its own native talents such as Nina Hagen.

8 January 1947
Born David Robert Jones in Brixton, London. Family move to Beckenham, where Bowie spends his formative years

1969
Years of unsuccessful single releases end when 'Space Oddity' reaches number five on the UK singles chart

1972
Unveils his Ziggy Stardust character, beginning four decades of inspiration

1973
Releases *Aladdin Sane* as Bowie 'retires' his Ziggy persona

1975
Ventures into soul music with *Young Americans*, increasing his US audience in the process

1976
Most successful film role as *The Man Who Fell to Earth*

1977
Low and *Heroes* albums (with *Lodger* (1979) part of his 'Berlin trilogy'), initiate electronic fusion

1983
Returns to mainstream pop with *Let's Dance*

2016
Releases *Blackstar*

10 January 2016
Dies in New York City, two days after his 69th birthday

DAVID BOWIE

Esteemed as the most important single UK rock artist, David Bowie's career was remarkable for its variety and durability. Beginning as a pop-mad youngster in the 1960s London suburbs, Bowie went through a number of unsuccessful groups, such as the Kon-Rads, the Manish Boys and the King Bees, concentrating mainly on cover material. He persevered for five years as a professional musician before landing his first hit, the self-written 'Space Oddity' in 1969. Relatively unsuccessful but much-loved albums – *The Man Who Sold the World* (1970), *Hunky Dory* (1971) – followed. However, it was 1972's launch of the bisexual, alien rock star with the LP *The Rise & Fall of Ziggy Stardust & the Spiders from Mars* that confirmed Bowie's messianic status. *Aladdin Sane* (1973) saw a further role change while building on the Ziggy audience. The *Diamond Dogs* tour of 1974 upped the ante of rock performance, with Bowie employing a staggering confidence and array of theatrical pyrotechnics. *Young Americans* (1975) had Bowie toying with soul music, and broadening his American audience. A further personality change saw the emergence of the so-called 'Thin White Duke' for the 'Berlin trilogy' of albums, *Low* (1977), *Heroes* (1977) and *Lodger* (1979), which were hailed for their ground-breaking, modernistic sound.

Diversions into film and stage acting – the translucent alien in the film *The Man Who Fell to Earth* (1976) and a well-received performance on Broadway in the title role of *The Elephant Man* – occupied Bowie until he returned to the pop mainstream with *Let's Dance* in 1983. Collaborations with Queen, Iggy Pop, Lou Reed and the Pet Shop Boys saw Bowie still leading from the front. Emerging acts such as Suede, New Order, Morrissey and Radiohead cited Bowie as a major influence. Constant role-playing, and a willingness to take risks, ensured perennial fascination.

Latterly Bowie enjoyed fewer hits, but stunning performances at Live Aid in 1985 and the Freddie Mercury Tribute concert (1992) testified to his stature. His skill was balancing commercial success alongside avant-garde experimentation. As a fashion icon, Bowie also played a seismic role, from the glam rock shock of the 1970s through to the cool chic of the twenty-first century. After years of silence, the albums *The Next Day* (2010) and *Blackstar* (2016) – the latter released just days before his death – were launched without fanfare, but were rapturously received. Whole generations testified to Bowie's influence on pop culture, style and music, and his death in 2016 was front-page news worldwide.

Patrick Humphries

MELBOURNE

the 30-second rock

In the early days of Australia's Beatles-inspired pop scene, acts such as the Bee Gees and the Easybeats gravitated to Sydney, but Melbourne soon became the major music centre as the young country forged a more confident and independent identity. In 1972 the flagship label Mushroom Records was established in the city, and scored a major success in 1975 with their signing of Skyhooks, the biggest-selling band in Australia up to that time. But their most notable success was perhaps with the art rockers Split Enz, whose Finn brothers, Tim and Neil, went on to form the nucleus of the internationally successful Crowded House, formed in 1985. Melbourne continued to attract some of the country's top talents; Paul Kelly made his first big impact there with his band The Dots in the mid-1970s, while The Sports were another local act who had national success in the new wave era. But artistically perhaps the most important rock figure to emerge was Nick Cave, originally with the Birthday Party and subsequently as Nick Cave and the Bad Seeds. Kylie Minogue is the light pop antithesis to Cave's dark gothic imagination, but the two Melburnians did unite in 1996 to record the hit single 'Where the Wild Roses Grow'.

RELATED TOPICS
See also
PUNK & NEW WAVE
page 46

INDIE & ALT-ROCK
page 50

GLAM ROCK
page 102

3-SECOND BIOGRAPHIES
MICHAEL GUDINSKI
1952–
Founder of Mushroom Records and leading Melbourne musical entrepreneur

PAUL KELLY
1955–
Australia's foremost singer-songwriter

NICK CAVE
1957–
Performer and writer, dubbed rock's 'Prince of Darkness'

30-SECOND TEXT
Hugh Weldon

Nick Cave cut his musical teeth on the Melbourne scene, but Kylie's pop and Kelly's songs have also been notable features.

3-SECOND LICK
Long regarded as Australia's cultural capital, Melbourne over the past four decades has developed into a truly global musical city.

3-MINUTE JAM
Late 1970s Melbourne was notable for a lively post-punk 'Little Band Scene' centred in the inner suburbs of Fitzroy and St Kilda; the leading club was Bombay Rock, which hosted many national and international acts before its closure in 1991. In the twenty-first century the scene is flourishing, with small music bars and clubs thriving, while major acts play top concert venues like the Hamer Hall or occasionally the 100,000-capacity Melbourne Cricket Ground.

REYKJAVÍK

the 30-second rock

The sounds of Iceland have a tone and a timbre that owe as much to the country's native mythology and unique landscape as they do to Anglo-Saxon traditions. Rock and pop were first heard here via the US Navy's radio station, and home-grown groups formed in the 1960s, one of which, Hljómar (later known as Thor's Hammer), recorded on the Beatles' label Parlophone. The Sugarcubes were the first band from Reykjavík to break through to international recognition; their lead singer Björk went on to a successful solo career, but she is perhaps only the best known of a range of performers from the capital who manage to sound both absolutely contemporary and rootedly Nordic. The atmospheric prog rock sounds of Sigur Rós, and the ethereal moods of Múm, can sound as typical of Reykjavík as the jazz funk of Mezzoforte or the Icelandic reggae of Hjálmar. The 2000 film *101 Reykjavik*, for which Icelandophile and Blur frontman Damon Albarn wrote the soundtrack, was instrumental in promoting both the city and the country to a global audience; the Kaffibarinn bar which appeared in the film is still a firm fixture of the city's nightlife.

RELATED TOPICS
See also
ELECTRO-ROCK
page 48

INDIE & ALT-ROCK
page 50

LANDMARK GIGS
page 70

3-SECOND BIOGRAPHIES
SIGTRYGGUR BALDURSSON
1962–
Singer, drummer and composer with many bands, director of Iceland Music Export

BJÖRK
1965–
Singer, actress, songwriter, vocalist with The Sugarcubes and subsequently solo artist

NANNA BRYDÍS HILMARSDÓTTIR
1989–
Joint lead vocalist with Of Monsters and Men, Iceland's top group of the twenty-first century

30-SECOND TEXT
Hugh Weldon

Björk's singular talents flourished against the backdrop of Iceland's singular landscape.

3-SECOND LICK
Reykjavík's impact on the global music scene since the 1990s has been remarkable for a city of only 123,000 people.

3-MINUTE JAM
Reykjavík's live music scene is concentrated in the small bars and clubs on or close to the main street Laugavegur. 12 Tónar on nearby Skólavörðustígur is a well-known record store that also operates its own label. Iceland Airwaves, held annually in November, has developed into a five-day festival of global prominence. And the city now has a major world-class venue with the architecturally imposing 1,800-capacity Harpa concert hall, which opened in 2011.

TOKYO
the 30-second rock

Tokyo first announced itself to the post-war world with the 1964 Olympic Games, whose theme tune 'Tokyo Melody' was a UK top ten hit; but a year earlier, Kyu Sakamoto had scored a US number one with 'Sukiyaki', a rare achievement for a non-English-language song. Tokyo-based artists continued to attract overseas attention in subsequent decades; Sadistic Mika Band made a UK impact in the glam mid-1970s, and The Plastics made a brief splash in the US in the new wave era that followed. But from the folk rock of Happy End to the quirky electronics of Yellow Magic Orchestra, a Japanese tradition evolved which culminated in the still-continuing J-pop phenomenon, a totally indigenous take on what had formerly been a very English-dominated genre. Tokyo acts such as Crystal Lake and Mr Children rather than Cheap Trick are now 'live at the Budokan' or 'big in Japan'. The Shibuya district, with its many clubs and bars, remains the centre of Tokyo's musical nightlife, and Tokyo-based Sony is now, fittingly, the second-largest music company in the world.

RELATED TOPICS
See also
PUNK & NEW WAVE
page 46

ELECTRO-ROCK
page 48

GLAM ROCK
page 102

3-SECOND BIOGRAPHIES
RYUICHI SAKAMOTO
1952–
Multi-talented musician with the Yellow Magic Orchestra, composer for films

YUMI MATSUTOYA
1954–
Singer, songwriter, one of Japan's leading female performers

YASUSHI AKIMOTO
1958–
Record producer, lyricist, television writer, responsible for AKB48, the Japanese 'idol' girl group phenomenon

30-SECOND TEXT
Hugh Weldon

While much of Tokyo's talent remains home based in its appeal, some artists have made a global impact.

3-SECOND LICK
Saké and Suntory, karaoke and manga: the pulsating neon-lit centre of a wider conurbation of 37 million people, Tokyo is the rocking heart of the Far East.

3-MINUTE JAM
The Nippon Budokan, originally built to house the Olympic martial arts competitions in 1964, is the city's largest and best-known venue, not least because of the number of best-selling live albums that have been recorded there, by Bob Dylan and others. Shibuya and the edgier Shinjuku are the top areas for clubs and small venues. Liquidroom in Ebisu is a long established and now more up-market club, that is often described as 'legendary'.

RESOURCES

BOOKS

*The Ambient Century: From Mahler to Moby –
The Evolution of Sound in the Electronic Age*
Mark Prendergast
(Bloomsbury, 2003)

*Awopbopaloobop Alopbambboom:
Pop from the Beginning*
Nik Cohn
(Vintage Classics, 2016)

The Complete Beatles Chronicle
Mark Lewisohn
(Pyramid, 1992)

The Complete David Bowie
Nicholas Pegg
(Titan Books, 2011)

Country
Nick Tosches
(Secker & Warburg, 1989)

Girl Groups
Alan Betrock
(Delilah, 1982)

Entertain Us: The Rise of Nirvana
Gillian G. Gaar
(Jawbone Press, 2012)

The Illustrated Encyclopedia of Music
Various authors
(Flame Tree, 2003)

John Varvatos: Rock in Fashion
John Varvatos and Holly George-Warren
(Harper Design, 2013)

Loser: The Real Seattle Music Story
Clark Humphrey
(Misc Media, 2016)

*Manchester: Looking for the Light
through the Pouring Rain*
Kevin Cummins
(Faber & Faber, 2012)

*No Direction Home: The Life & Music
of Bob Dylan*
Robert Shelton; revised and updated by
Elizabeth Thomson & Patrick Humphries
(Omnibus Press, 2011)

*Nothing But the Blues: The Music
and the Musicians.*
Various authors
(Abbeville Press, 1993)

*Rock of Ages: The Rolling Stone History
of Rock & Roll*
Ed Ward, Geoffrey Stokes and Ken Tucker
(Summit Books, 1986)

The Sound of the City
Charlie Gillett
(Sphere Books, 1971)

Vinyl: The Art of Making Records
Mike Evans
(Aurum, 2015)

WEBSITES

www.allmusic.com

www.discogs.com

www.charliegillett.com

www.rockmusictimeline.com

www.rocksbackpages.com

www.rollingstone.com

ultimateclassicrock.com

www.wired.co.uk

FESTIVALS

USA
Lollapalooza, Chicago (August)
www.lollapalooza.com

Bonnaroo, Manchester, Tennessee (June)
www.bonnaroo.com

Coachella Valley, California (April)
www.coachella.com

Europe
Glastonbury, UK (June)
www.glastonburyfestivals.co.uk

Reading/Leeds, UK (August)
www.readingfestival.com

Roskilde, Denmark (June–July)
www.roskilde-festival.dk

EXIT, Novi Sad, Serbia (July)
www.exifest.org/en

Asia
Wonderfruit, Pattaya, Thailand (February)
www.wonderfruitfestival.com

FujiRock, Naeba, Japan (July)
fujirock-eng.com

Australasia
Rhythm and Vines, Gisborne, New Zealand
(December)
www.rhythmandvines.co.nz

Byron Bay Bluesfest, NSW, Australia (Easter)
www.bluesfest.com.au

NOTES ON CONTRIBUTORS

EDITOR
Mike Evans A musician on the 1960s rock scene, Mike began writing about popular music in the 1970s. As a freelance writer he was a regular contributor to *Melody Maker*, and since the late 1980s, has worked in book publishing, commissioning and editing titles on popular culture. As an author his books on music have included the much-acclaimed *The Art of the Beatles* in 1984, the best-selling *Elvis: A Celebration* (2002) and *Ray Charles: The Birth of Soul* in 2005. *Woodstock: Three Days That Rocked the World* appeared in 2009, *The Blues: A Visual History* in 2014 and *Vinyl: The Art of Making Records* in 2015.

CONTRIBUTORS
Gillian G. Gaar has written for numerous publications, including *Mojo*, *Rolling Stone* and *Goldmine*. Her previous books include *She's a Rebel: The History of Women in Rock & Roll*, *Entertain Us: The Rise of Nirvana*, *Return of the King: Elvis Presley's Great Comeback* and *Green Day: Rebels with a Cause*, among others. She served as a Project Consultant for Nirvana's *With the Lights Out* box set. She lives in Seattle.

Patrick Humphries began his writing career as a 'hip young gunslinger' on *NME* back in the last century. Since then, he has written over a dozen musical biographies, including definitive works on Nick Drake, Richard Thompson and Lonnie Donegan.

Paul Kingsbury is a writer and editor living in Nashville, Tennessee. He has written books about the Grand Ole Opry radio programme, the historic Hatch Show Print letterpress poster shop and the history of country music album covers. He has edited several multi-author books including *The Encyclopedia of Country Music* and *Country Music: The Complete Visual History*. With Mike Evans, he co-wrote *Woodstock: Three Days That Rocked the World*. His articles on music have appeared in *Entertainment Weekly*, *US Weekly*, *American Songwriter*, *Country Music*, *The Journal of Country Music*, *Guitar World Acoustic* and numerous other publications.

Spencer Leigh has hosted his *On The Beat* programme on BBC Radio Merseyside for over 30 years,. He has written several books on the Beatles as well as biographies of Frank Sinatra, Simon and Garfunkel and Elvis Presley.

Hugh Weldon was born in Liverpool, just a little too early for the Beatles and Merseybeat, but grew up with a passion for pop and rock that was ignited further by the punk and new wave scene that flourished around the legendary Eric's club in the late 1970s. The major part of his career has been in education, as a teacher and educational administrator, though he has contributed to various publications on educational and other topics. He currently works at a community library in North London.

INDEX

ACKNOWLEDGEMENTS

PICTURE CREDITS

The publisher would like to thank the following for permission to reproduce copyright material:

Alamy/Everett Collection Inc: 79BL, 86, 105C, 127C; Granamour Weems Collection: 29BL, 71BL, 103BC; Grenville Charles: 133C; Joe Bird: 131C; Keystone Pictures USA: 145CR; Marka: 40; Moviestore Collection: 26; Photo 12: 146; Pictorial Press Ltd: 23TL, 23BR, 63T, 97TC, 103TC, 117C, 123C, 143CR, 145TC; Ric Carter: 17TR; Trinity Mirror/Mirrorpix: 77C, 83TL, 139C; World History Archive: 31BL; ZUMA Press, Inc.: 49C.
Flickr/British Library: 143BR; David Sikes: 91C; Drew de F Fawkes: 151CR; Eric Hossinger: 85TR; James Dennes: 145CL; kingArthur_aus/Bruce: 149TC; Provincial Archives of Alberta: 7CR, 37CR.
Getty/Allan Tannenbaum: 85TC; Bettman: 64; Chris Mills: 143TC; Chris Walter/WireImage: 45TC; Kevin.Mazur/INACTIVE/WireImage: 45BC; Koh Hasebe/Shinko Music: 109CL; Lindsay Brice: 149TC; Martyn Goodacre: 91CR(BG); Michael Ochs Archives: 9TC, 59TC, 99TC, 119C; Michael Putland: 43TC, 43BC; Michel Linssen/Redferns: 109CR; Mick Hutson/Redferns: 51T; Paul Natkin: 51B; Peter Pakvis/Redferns: 141TC; Photoshot: 124; Popperfoto: 63C; Raffaella Cavalieri/Redferns: 129C; Santiago Felipe: 151TC.
Library of Congress, Washington DC/Al Aumuller: 39C; Carol M. Highsmith: 117CL(BG), 145C, 145BC; Fred Palumbo: 31TR; James Kavallines: 123B; James R. Lockhart: 69CR(BG); John Vachon: 31TL; Lomax Collection: 17BL; Marion Post Walcott: 17BR; Marion S. Trikosko: 71TC; Prints and Photographs Division: 117R(BG), 117L(BG), 139CR, 139C(BG), 139C, 141TR; Russell Lee: 23TR; William P. Gottlieb Collection: 19BL, 21TL, 21TC, 25TC, 25BR, 89TL, 133TR.
Nationaal Archief, Netherlands/Bert Verhoeff: 71CR, 77TR; Rob Bogaerts: 89TR, 111TR; Eric Koch: 7CL, 11BR, 37CL, 83BC, 99C, 121C, 121CL; Fotograaf Onbekend: 19TC, 21CR, 111CL; Harry Pot: 111TL, 111CR; Hugo van Gelderen: 7C, 37C, 39BL; Jac. de Nijs: 101TCL, 101TCR, 139TC, 139TL; Joop van Bilsen: 67TR; Joost Evers: 77C, 89BC; Koen Suyk: 47C, 143CL; Marcel Antonisse: 69CL; Ron Kroon: 39TR, 101BC.
National Archives Catalog/Department of Defense. Department of the Navy. U.S. Marine Corps: 85C(BG), 85CR(BG); Rowland Scherman: 119 TR(BG).
Shutterstock/Aanush: 103BC; Aaron Kohr: 45C; Agsandrew: 43T(BG); AKaiser: 67BL; Aleks_DT: 131BL, 139BL; Alexsandar Grozdanovski: 2C, 57C; Alexander Lysenko: 151BC; A Luna Blue: 49B; ALEXEY FILATOV: 9BC, 59BC; AlexHiiv: 105TR; Alted Studio: 123C(BG); Alym Design: 127(BG); AmySachar: 127(BG); Ana Pavao: 103C; Anastasia Mazeina: 77TR; Andrea Raffi: 153C; Andreas Gradin: 45CL, 45CR; Andrey Shinkov: 45C(BG); Anita Ponne: 61C; Anna Grishenko: 133TC; Anno: 153(BG); Antishock: 143(BG); ArgelisRebolledo: 151TC; Athos Boncompagni Illustratore: 143R; Atlaspix: 109C; Axro: 9BL, 59BL, 61C; Bardocz Peter: 69(BG); Ba_peuceta: 9TR, 59TR; Be Good: 81C; BeautyImage: 119CL; BNMK0819: 63B; Boris Znaev: 19C(BG); Bulbspark: 39C(BG) 67CL; Café Racer: 51; Cesare Cartoon: 85CR; CHAINFOTO24: 63CR; Chatdanai Dorkson: 151CL; Chrisbrignel: 7C(BG), 37C(BG); Chrisdorney: 121T; Chris Green: 121CR; Christi 180884: 2BR, 57BR; Cla78: 91(BG); Cvijovic Zarko: 45TL, 45BR; Danyliuk Konstantine 23BR(BG); Darren Pullman: 81C; Dave Allen Photography: 21TC; Dexterous simpson: 61TC; Diana Piccaluga: 143TL; Dimitris_k: 67C; Dinga: 23BR(BG); Donatas 1205: 81TC, 121CL; DutchScenery: 7BC, 31C, 37BC; Echo3005: 47TR; Elivagar: 105TC; Everett Collection: 29TR; FARBAI: 141CL; Fat Jackey: 121CL; Featureflash Photo Agency: 99BC, 149BR; Fer Gregory: 25C; Finlandi: 145BC; Friendwithlove: 39TL(BG), 67CL; Fukurou: 111CL; GaryKillian: 91C; God rick: 25TR(BG); Gordan: 43C; GrashAlex: 2BR, 57BR; Gritsalak karalak: 153BR; Grop: 105TR; Gyvafoto: 105BC; HANA: 25CL; IM_photo: 153BC; Indigolotos: 61C; I.Pilon: 21B; Iulias: 43BR; James Steid: 79TR; Jannoon028: 81BR; Janpen Boonbao: 17C(BG), 29BR, 45TC, 47BR, 51BR; Jason Winter: 139B; Jim Pruitt: 21TR; Joachim Wendler: 121BC; Johann Helgason: 151BC; JohnJohnson: 141BL, 141BC; Juan Roballo: 91TL; K. Narloch-Liberra: 133BC; Kaponia Aliaksei: 31C; KOZYREV OLEG: 85BL; Krasovski Dmitri: 109C; Kristen Hinte: 9TL(BG), 59(BG); Larina Marina: 105C; LazarevDN: 105BL; Levgenii Meyer: 45C; LiliGraphie: 105C; Lora liu: 39TL; Luciano Queiroz: 10BL, 21CL; Lukas Gojda: 25TR; Magdelena Kucova: 9C, 59C; Makalo86: 63T; Mark Grenier: 61TR; Martin Gardeazabal: 129CR; Mato: 145TL; Maxger: 49C; Maximillian Laschon: 45CR; M.E. Mulder: 121CL; Mervas: 97T; Mexrix: 85C; Michaket: 25CR; MigrenArt: 111TR; Militarist: 117BR; Mircea Pavel: 119CR; Miqu77: 83CL; Mr Aesthetics: 19BR(BG); MSSA: 19TL(BG); Nerthuz: 19TR(BG); Nicku: 19TC(BG); NirdalArt: 143C; Nne: 153(BG); Northfoto: 106BL; NosorogUA: 99TC; NoSpoon Design: 127(BG); Oksana2010: 149TC; Optimark: 9C, 59C, 61C, 78C; OSSEYFFER: 91(BG); Pablo Scapinachis: 79B; Pbombaert: 17C(BG); Pensiri: 9BC, 59BC; Perekotypole: 99C; Persero8888: 97(BG); Petr Lerch: 123C; Petr Malyshev: 97(BG); Photopixel: 81C; Picsfive: 67TR; Plasteed: 89(BG); Policas: 69CL; Practicuum: 103TC; PrinceOfLove: 91C; Railway tx: 149BC; RedHead_Anna: 47CR; RemarkEliza: 10BL, 21BR; Rlassman: 131T; RLRRLRLL: 21BC; RRuntsch: 141TR; RuleByArt: 91(BG); SA Production: 49CL; Sam DCruz : 153CL; Sandy MacKenzie: 43BL; Sanit Fuangnakhon: 69CL; Sbarabu: 29CR; Sculpies: 85CR; Sean Pavone: 111C; Sergey Nivens: 29TR; Shipowner: 2C, 57C; Shiva3d: 45BL, 45BR; Silvano audisio: 49B(BG); Siloto: 131C(BG); Sirtravelalot: 83C; SPbPhoto: 17CL(BG); Stephen Coburn: 129TL; Steve Collender: 47TR; Steven Rees: 81TR; Steven Wright: 23CR(BG); SvedOliver: 63B; Surin Sergey: 97(BG); SurfsUp: 89C; Taig: 79(BG); Tania Anisimova: 77BL; Thawornnurak: 61TC; Thomas Pajot: 143R; Tofutyklein: 121(BG); TotemArt: 45CL; Transia Design: 121BC; Trekandshoot: 2TL, 10TR, 31TR, 57T; TRINACRIA PHOTO: 2C, 57C; Trubavin: 97C; Twin Design: 7(BG), 37(BG); VAlex: 91C; Vector.design: 143TR; Vereshchagin Dmitry: 10BL, 21C; Victorian Traditions: 25TL; Vnlit: 77(BG); Wavebreakmedia: 29TC.
Wikipedia/Gorupdebesanez: 79TL; Gus Pasquerella: 61TL; Lisa Moran Parker: 79CR(BG); Media History Digital Library: 99T; Mika Väisänen: 139CR; Misterweiss: 63CL; National Archives and Records Administration/Rowland Scherman: 39TC, 71TL; Pismo: 47TC Roland Godefroy: 19CR, 67TR; Rowland Scherman: 67BL, 85CL, 85BL; State Library Victoria: 149C(BG); Wikimedia Commons: 131TL.

All reasonable efforts have been made to trace copyright holders and to obtain their permission for the use of copyright material. The publisher apologizes for any errors or omissions in the list above and will gratefully incorporate any corrections in future reprints if notified.